Bootle Milestones

People, places and events in Bootle's history

RESPICE·ASPICE·PROSPICE

by Roy Redman & Colin Sands

Illustrated

 SEFTON LIBRARIES

Uniform with this volume, by the same authors, "Bootle Signposts: a history and directory of Bootle streets"

2006
Published by Sefton Council
Leisure Services Department (Libraries)
Pavilion Buildings, 99-105 Lord Street
Southport PR8 1RH

ISBN 1-874516-15-4

Printed in Great Britain by **Mitchell & Wright Printers Limited**, The Print Works, Banastre Road, Southport PR8 5AL   Tel. **01704 535529**

Preface

Welcome to Bootle Milestones, a kaleidoscope of interesting facts, figures and events culled from a wide variety of sources and presented here for you to explore. Whether you are recalling days past or simply enjoy trivia we hope that you will find much of interest and enjoyment between these pages. We have not sought to provide a comprehensive history of the town but rather to highlight some of the interesting events, major and minor, that have occurred over the centuries. Our sources include Council minutes, local newspapers, Diocesan and Archdiocesan records, directories and publications by other local historians. Together these snapshots plot the changing character of the town through the decades.

Bootle first emerged on record as a settlement around the year 613. It appeared in the Domesday Survey of 1086, an honour not shared by its bigger neighbour Liverpool! From the inception of Bootle as a Borough in 1868, Liverpool made many attempts to absorb the town into its own boundaries. Bootle was always fiercely independent and its inhabitants were delighted when the last attempt by Liverpool failed in 1903, prompting the Mayor, Alderman Clemmey's dramatic telegram from London proclaiming 'Thank God we've won'.

The name Bootle, in its various guises, appears in official records a number of times prior to the start of the 19th century. Here to record a change of ownership, there to record the appointment of a minor official. It is not however until the dawn of the eighteen hundreds that there is a significant increase in the number of events recorded. Bootle in 1841 had a population of less than 2,000 and was described as a 'small quiet watering place'. However by the end of the century it had become a vibrant, active, bustling Borough dominated by dockyards and heavy industry, with a population that had mushroomed to over 58,000. This growth witnessed an influx of people seeking employment. Entrepreneurs, eager to exploit the business opportunities to be found in the thriving Borough were also attracted to the town. It is possible in fact to identify 75 different industries active in the area by the beginning of the 20th century.

In 1841 St. Mary's Anglican Church, a Chapel of Ease to the parish church of Walton, was the only place of worship in the locality. During the century the influx of people, many with Scottish, Welsh or Irish roots, saw the establishment of churches of multifarious denominations. Many of the new churches had their beginnings in attic rooms, stables and people's homes until the finances were raised to build permanent church buildings.

Prior to 1835, when St. Mary's National School was built, education was in the hands of small private schools that operated in the teachers' homes. The Roman Catholic community founded their first school (St. James) in 1848 and others followed. With the establishment of the School Board in 1870 the local community provided non-denominational schools, of which Bedford Road and Salisbury Road schools were the first examples.

After the creation of Bootle as a Borough, and until the start of the Second World War, the townspeople had a very active social calendar. Community leaders and local business people were actively engaged in philanthropic works. Numerous societies, many with charitable aims, were established and provided much needed support to the community especially during the years of the 'Great Depression'. Probably the most significant innovation was the establishment of the Annual May Day celebrations that raised funds for the hospital and other local charities. Many of these societies feature in our book, as do accounts of how the people of Bootle celebrated local and national events and welcomed their own and foreign monarchs to the Borough.

The Second World War was a time of great suffering for the people of Bootle as they endured regular bombing by the Luftwaffe. Much destruction occurred and many lives were lost. Post-war the town rose from the ashes as new office blocks were built, the New Strand shopping complex was opened and housing developments in the north of the Borough in Netherton and Sefton provided much needed homes.

The result of all our research has, we hope, created an interesting mine of information that our readers can dig into again and again. Whilst we have made very effort to be accurate with names and dates we apologise if sources have occasionally provided data that may be open to query. We have found it particularly difficult to locate and confirm the names of nonconformist ministers due to the lack of central records. If you feel that we have omitted something important please feel free to contact us. Finally we have included as an appendix a listing of all known headteachers, ministers of religion, council officials, May Queens etc in the Borough over the years.

Roy Redman and Colin Sands,
November 2006

Bootle The Beginning, A.D. 613 - 1800

Bootle's history dates back to Anglo Saxon times and the name itself is a clue to how long people have been living in the area, for it comes from the Anglo Saxon word 'bold' or 'botl' which means a dwelling place. In the Domesday survey of 1086 Bootle is referred to as 'Boltelai'. The dwelling that gave its name to the town is thought to have stood in the area now known as Bankhall.

The late Arthur Hardman, a former Bootle Librarian and local historian, suggested that the village might have been established by some of the victorious Anglians who remained on Merseyside after their King Aethelfrith had won a battle at Chester in A.D.613. Raghanald, a descendant of one of the Norsemen who had settled in this part of the country, was possibly one of the four thanes recorded in the Domesday survey. His grandson Roger was the first recorded Lord of the Manor of Bootle. Through marriage in 1200, the Bootle estates passed into the hands of the Beetham family of Westmorland. The Beethams held Bootle until 1485 when, again as a result of marriage, the Middleton family of Leighton in Yealand (then in Yorkshire but now in Lancashire) acquired the Manor.

It was George Middleton who, in 1566, parted with the Manor and Lordship of Bootle for the princely sum of £570 to John Moore of Bankhall. His descendant and namesake John Moore, became M.P. for Bootle and served in the Long Parliament. He is best remembered as one of the signatories on the execution warrant of King Charles I in 1648. It was his son Sir Cleave Moore who sold the Estates and Manor of Bootle to James 10th Earl of Derby for £14,000 in 1724. From that time the Earls of Derby played a major part in Bootle's story.

Documents relating to Bootle in the 17th and 18th centuries reveal it to be largely a waste of barren sandhills and marshes around the shore of Bootle Bay with a few scattered fishermen's huts and cottages. This reveals a rural area where local residents faced poverty and hardship. Court records from this period record, for example that Edward Lunt of Litherland was found guilty in 1626 of stealing bird traps from near Bootle watermill, while in 1628 a conspiracy to steal corn from John Munch of Bootle was uncovered. Quarter sessions records from 1629-30 also record assaults being made on Miles Wadington, who was the Constable of Bootle - an office of ancient origin.

Another grim reminder of what life could be like in 17th century Bootle was the visitation of the plague, which raged in the area from 1652-53. It is recorded that on June 12th 1652 William Robinson, a male servant, was the first person in Bootle to die of the plague. How many people succumbed to the outbreak is not known but it was severe enough for a petition to be made to the County Justices sitting at the Quarter Session in Ormskirk seeking financial help for the stricken village in its hour of need.

Some of the family names recorded in these early years are still familiar in Bootle today. It was a Thomas Beri, after whom Berry Street is named, who in 1601 founded the Beri charity that paid for the distribution of free loaves of bread to three deserving Bootle families each Sunday. Another local name, Musker, appears in Bootle records as early as the 16th century. In 1750 a James Musker was appointed Constable of Bootle and his duties included the recruiting of a militia, escorting felons to court and maintaining the stocks. It was a descendant, Joseph Musker, who was a member of the deputation that went to London to obtain the Borough's Charter in 1868. The family continued to play a role in public life well into the 20th century and are remembered in Musker Drive.

By the end of the 18th century Bootle - which could be reached from Liverpool either by hackney carriage for a cost of 5/- or by a 45-minute canal journey at a cost of 8d - remained a rural backwater. However, it had two coffeehouses: it was here that travellers on the canal and country folk taking their produce to market in Liverpool could rest awhile and take some refreshment. In addition during the summer months visitors flocked to the area to enjoy the recuperative benefits of sea bathing in Bootle Bay. The attraction of the place was such that a number of Liverpool merchants built their villas along the shore. In 1773 Lord Derby had a hunting lodge built in Bootle village: the building survives to this day as Number One Merton Road. Stables for the lodge were built in Litherland Road: they, too, have survived and currently house a small printing company.

In 1797 the Bootle Water Company was established to extract water from the Bootle Springs and in 1799 water from the wells was supplied to Liverpool for the first time.

The years of the 19th and 20th century, here chronicled, record some of the events that contributed to the growth of Bootle from a quiet, rustic village into a bustling, industrial town.

1801

- The first decennial census showed 537 people living in Bootle.
- Bootle's pure spring water had by this time attracted many small industries e.g. bleaching, tanning and papermaking to the area.

1802

- The Jawbone Public House in Litherland Road was opened.

1807

- H.R.H. the Duke of Gloucester visited Bootle Bay on September 14th to review the militia and volunteers.

1808

- On the instruction of the town council a new chest was made to hold the town's books, papers etc. and the said chest was deposited in the Constable's hands. The chest was not to be opened except in the presence of the Constable.

1811

- The Census recorded 102 houses and a population of 610 residents living in Bootle. Of the 107 families, 32 were employed in agriculture and 52 in trade and manufacturing.

1813

- The Bootle Water Company was now supplying water to Bootle, Kirkdale, Everton, West Derby, Walton-on-the-Hill and Liverpool.

1816

- The Leeds Liverpool Canal Company doubled the width of the Coffee House Bridge.

1819

- A public meeting of the townspeople was held at the Sign of the Bull in Bootle on March 29th The Constable was authorised to have a stone building constructed at a cost of no more than £30 to serve as a temporary bridewell.

1821

- Census: the population of Bootle is recorded as 808.

1822

- The administration of all legal matters pertaining to Bootle, including the swearing in of Justices, was transferred from the Justices at Ormskirk Quarter Sessions to the Justices at Kirkdale.

1823

- Great storms drove vessels on to the shores of Bootle Bay on March 4th.
- Eighty children were on the books of the Baptist Sunday School. Eight teachers taught the children, with Mr Lloyd as the Superintendent.

1824

- William Spurstow Miller, a Liverpool solicitor, purchased a piece of land near the seashore close to what is now Miller's Bridge, and built a castellated stone mansion known as 'Miller's Castle'.

1827

- The Bishop of Chester consecrated St Mary's C of E Church in Derby Road on May 10th as a Chapel of Ease to St Mary's Walton-on-the-Hill. It had twin towers that were used by mariners as navigational aids as they made their way up the Mersey estuary. The builder was a Mr Eyes, and William Spurstow Miller met the building costs. The first incumbent was the Rev. John Gladstone who served until 1846. He was a relative of the family of William Ewart Gladstone who was later to become Prime Minister. The vicarage at this time was in Seaview Road.
- On August 26th the registers in St Mary's Church recorded entries for the first time: the burial in the churchyard of four-month-old Elizabeth Hopkins and the baptism of Robert Thomson Gladstone, son of Hugh and Margaret Gladstone.

B565

1. Bootle Bay, looking towards Liverpool.
This view dates from 1835, but the Bootle shore would have appeared much the same in the preceding centuries.

1829

- Two great obelisks, 100-feet high with conical tops and mounted on massive stone steps, were constructed on the Bootle foreshore. They appear in a painting by Samuel Austin (1796-1834) to be seen in the Walker Art Gallery, Liverpool. These obelisks along with the tower of St George's Church in Everton served as landmarks to guide ships into port. At low tide the stone steps were a popular place for local children to play. The landmarks were removed in the 1860s.

1830

- The first horse-drawn omnibus service between Liverpool and Bootle commenced on May 12th. Two services ran to Bootle: one to Kirkdale Station (then known as Bootle Lane Station) and one to the Tollhouse on Derby Road.
- The Bridge Inn close to the canal in Litherland Road was opened.

1831

- The census showed the population of Bootle to be 1,133.

1832

- Following a meeting held on March 26th at the residence of Mr Webster of Linacre, a rate of 6d in the pound was levied on the township of Bootle for the purpose of the erection of St Mary's School in Irlam Road. The Earl of Derby provided the land on which the school was to be built as a gift.
- A Sunday School was started in Bootle village by a group of people belonging to the Presbyterian Church of Wales. This was to be the nucleus of what later became the congregation of the church built on the corner of Stanley and Trinity Roads and opened in 1861.

1833

- Bootle Cricket Club was founded and played on land in Irlam Road where it remained until 1883.

1834

- Shaw's windmill in Bootle, one of the oldest in the Liverpool area, was destroyed by fire on January 4th. There had been a mill on the site for over 200 years.
- Shaw's Directory of Liverpool and its Environs for 1834 refers to 'Bootle Hall', which at the time was the residence of the Irlam family, after whom Irlam Road is named.

1835

- As a result of the 1833 Lighting and Watching Act a meeting of local ratepayers was held on September 11th in the Derby Arms Hotel, Irlam Road. The meeting decided to establish a Watch Committee consisting of twelve inspectors, to see to the watching and lighting of the town, and to acquire a fire engine. (Before police forces were established watchmen patrolled the streets, especially at night; lighting streets was also the job of the watchmen, who carried lanterns to guide people to their homes. A fire engine consisted of a cart

PA6-23

2. Bootle Church and Landmarks.
1832, showing how small the township was. St. Mary's Church was opened in 1827; the two landmarks were built 1829 and demolished in the 1860s.

dragged by either men or horses, and bearing a very simple pump and a supply of leather buckets). Subsequently handbills were circulated locally advertising for watchmen who had to be able-bodied and not older than thirty-five. On September 23rd Joseph Rowson was appointed Inspector of the Watch at a wage of 30/- per week. John Croft, Robert Parkinson, Thomas Almond and John Hudson were appointed watchmen at a wage of 15/- per week. The area to be watched was bounded as follows: on the east by the Leeds-Liverpool Canal, on the west by the River Mersey, on the south by the brook dividing the township of Bootle-cum-Linacre from Kirkdale and on the north by the lanes leading from Rimrose Bridge up Marsh Lane and then east to the canal. Watch was to be kept from 9 p.m. to 5 a.m. and the hours (time) were to be called regularly.

- St Mary's C of E School to accommodate 875 pupils was built in Irlam Road. The National Society established it initially as a Sunday School for 'The promoting of education to the poor in the principles of the established church'. The following year it became a day school and Mr H. Roberts was appointed Headmaster.
- Mr Patrick Donnelly was appointed Superintendent of the Watch in December.
- Clarence Dock was opened. It was named after William, Duke of Clarence who by this date had been crowned King William IV.

1837

- The West Derby Union created the Township of Bootle-cum-Linacre.

1839

- There was a severe storm on January 6th-7th and nine ships were wrecked on the Bootle strand (seashore).
- On November 6th, following the passing of the Rural Constabulary Act, the County Justices decided to appoint 500 constables to police the county of Lancashire. A chief constable was appointed who was to be paid £500 per year, two assistant chief constables (£200 per year each), 13 superintendents (£100 per year) and constables who would be paid 18/- weekly.
- The first Tithe Map of Bootle was drawn showing each piece of land, its size and the names of the owners and occupiers.

1840

- The Lancashire County Justices took over responsibility for policing Bootle on April 12th. Six Lancashire Constabulary police officers under the command of Captain John Woodford, the Chief Constable of the Lancashire force, were appointed to patrol Bootle. Duncan McRae, who is regarded as the father of Bootle's police force, was placed in charge. These constables replaced the existing part-time watchmen.
- John Bibby, a leading Bootle resident and founder of the Bibby shipping line, died in tragic circumstances on Linacre Marsh on July 16th. Bibby's Lane is named after him.
- The rateable value of Bootle was £12,462.

1841

- The first national census to contain personal details of the population was conducted in June. The census showed the population of Bootle to be 1,962.
- The first street lighting in Bootle was in Derby Road and went as far as Rimrose Bridge. The Liverpool Gas Company provided the gas at a cost of £2 10/- per lamp per year.
- The Tithe Apportionment for Bootle was completed in May. This enabled tithes to be commuted to rents based on the prevailing price of corn. Bootle consisted of 1,171 acres, of which the Earl of Derby owned almost 1,000 acres.

1844

- Derby Road Baptist Church was founded on the corner of Derby Road and Chapel Street with seating for 585. The congregation moved to a new church in Stanley Road in 1896.

1845

- The rateable value of Bootle was £15,625, the population was 3,184 and there were twenty constables on duty. By the following year the number of constables had doubled!
- St James' RC Church and School was built in St James' Place alongside the site of the future Marsh Lane Station. At this time the railway track was not raised, the track being crossed by a level crossing. (A mission church had been founded some years earlier, in a room on the left bank of the canal near Coffee House Bridge.) Father Henry Sharples was the first resident parish priest

- Bootle Education Institute was founded to provide the children of tradesmen and the working classes of the neighbourhood with a good practical education within the means of their parents. Evening classes were also provided for apprentices and mechanics at a rate of 6d per week.

3. St. James's RC Church   B494
Opened 1845, was Bootle's first Catholic church. This photograph probably dates from the 1860s or '70s.
A new building replaced this one in 1886.

1846

- The towers of St Mary's Church were destroyed by fire. The Earl of Derby paid for the towers to be replaced by a spire containing a clock and a bell. The two western bays of the aisle were also constructed increasing the capacity of the church to 1,500.
- The first dispensary in Bootle was established in the surgery of Dr Reid on the corner of Strand and Derby Roads. In the same year an inaugural meeting was held to form a committee to raise public subscriptions to build a hospital.

1847

- Thomas Sands laid the foundation stone of a Wesleyan Chapel in Sheridan Place. The Chapel was opened in 1848 the congregation having previously met in a room at the back of the Mersey Hotel in Derby Road.
- To facilitate the construction of the north docks Edward Smith Stanley, 13th Earl of Derby, sold 270,000 yards of the foreshore to the Mersey Dock Trust for £90,000.

1848

- Liverpool Corporation acquired Bootle Wells on March 1st for the sum of £294,087 9/-.
- St Mary's Church was licensed for marriages.
- The 'Dickie Sam' a schooner carrying a cargo of tobacco was shipwrecked on the Bootle foreshore. Local residents plundered the cargo!

1849

- The first Welsh Preaching Festival was held in the town.

1850

- Death of William Spurstow Miller, after whom Miller's Bridge is named. He was buried in St Mary's churchyard.
- Bootle boys were allowed to become pupils at Merchant Taylors' School in Crosby for the first time.
- 123 pupils were on the roll of St Mary's C of E School. Each child paid 2d per week towards the cost of their education.

1851

- The census taken on March 31st showed the population of Bootle to be 4,106.

1852

- In November the inhabitants of Bootle experienced two earthquakes.
- Samuel Walters, the marine artist came to live in Bootle, first at Falkner Terrace in Derby Road before moving to Merton Road.

1854

- Bootle was valued for assessing the county rate at £18,538.

1855

- Marriages were licensed in St James RC Church from January 8th.
- A Nuisances Removal Committee was elected on November 15th to arrange for the removal of effluvia (sewage) from houses and trade premises. Mr Joseph Musker was appointed the first Sanitary Inspector.
- A United Presbyterian preaching centre was opened in Derby Road next to the Mersey Hotel. It was built for the benefit of Scottish people living in Bootle who were dissatisfied with the existing provision.

B1338

4. Samuel Walters
Marine artist, came to live in Bootle in 1852 and died in the town in 1882.
(Photo courtesy Bootle Times)

1856

- A trial of Mr Whitworth's hexagonal gun took place on May 6th on the shore near Bootle. One of the balls weighing 24 lbs cut down a tree and entered the parlour window of a timber merchant living in Waterloo. There was damage to property but no one was hurt!
- The Huskisson Building Society was established in the Hand in Hand Club in Kirkdale. The society was founded with the intention of helping to finance the erection of dwellings in Bootle at a time of early development in the area. The head office was later moved to Stanley Road.

1858

- A Bootle girl, Mary Formby aged 11, stole a tablecloth. The Lancaster County Sessions Court ordered her imprisonment in a House of Correction with hard labour for 14 days. This was to be followed by a five-year sentence in a Reformatory School.
- A municipal fire brigade was established under the control of the Head Constable of Lancashire, Colonel Bruce. It consisted of one inspector and six constables.
- On August 10th there was a fire in Berry Street at midnight. The firemen could do little as the water was turned off 'as usual'!
- The group of Presbyterians that was later to establish the Bootle and Linacre Mission held meetings in a house in Bootle village and established a Sabbath School.
- A hospital for eight patients was established in a private house in Berry Street.

1859

- On July 26th William Forwood, the renowned Liverpool ship owner, watched from the Bootle foreshore as the 'Great Britain', the world's first large iron steam ship, made its way down the Mersey on its maiden voyage to New York.
- Canada Basin, the first dock in Bootle, was opened on September 15th. The first ship in the dock was the Cunard steamer 'Asia' which was captained by Captain Lott.
- Formation of the Bootle Dolphin Boat Club.
- Ford RC Cemetery, designed by W. J. Turner, was opened. On part of the land the Sisters of Charity opened the Convent of the Good Shepherd that contained a penitentiary for fallen women.

1860

- Rev. Dr Crighton laid the foundation stone of a Presbyterian Church in Derby Road on May 11th on the site of the Preaching Centre. The church could seat 940 people and cost £4,000.
- Jessie Hartley the Dock Engineer died in Bootle on August 24th. He was buried in St Mary's churchyard.
- Bootle and Linacre Mission obtained bigger premises in Laburnum Place. A Total Abstinence Society was established and the Sabbath School was expanded. Classes were now held on four evenings each week. Later a day school for 100 children was opened in Linacre under the tuition of Miss Sarah Parr.

1861

- The census taken on March 1st showed 6,414 people living in Bootle.
- Fifty-one dwellings in Dundas Street and Lyons Street were closed because of unsanitary conditions.
- A Presbyterian Church of Wales church was built on the corner of Stanley and Trinity Roads.

1862

- As a result of the 1862 Highway Act a Highway Board was set up to control road building and repairs and to provide street nameplates.
- The Canada Half-tide Basin, later Brocklebank Dock, was opened for the importation of timber.
- Merton Road, from Coffee House Bridge to Hawthorne Road was paved at a cost of £761 10/6d.
- Opening of the Welsh Calvinistic Methodist Church on the corner of Miller's Bridge and Brasenose Road.
- A Welsh Baptist group commenced meeting in Princes Terrace.
- The firm of James Webster and Bros. was established in Bootle and started to import timber.
- Bootle-cum-Linacre Mission was reorganised on undenominational lines, bringing to an end their contact with the Presbyterian Church.

1863

- The Bootle Cage Bird Society was founded.
- Bruce and Hyslop established a craft foundry in Park Street.

1864

- St John's C of E Church and Schools were opened on June 17th in Brasenose Road. The first incumbent was the Rev. R. W. Bardsley. The schools could accommodate 770 pupils. Mr Adam Kay was the first Headmaster.
- There was a severe outbreak of typhoid in the town.
- Work began on the building of Balliol Road Methodist Church on the corner of Balliol and Pembroke Roads. When it opened in 1866 it could accommodate 900 worshippers.
- The Victoria Beer Hall was opened at the corner of Regent Road and Howe Street. It is currently known as the Regent Hotel.
- Peter Hanlon of Bootle, aged 13, was sent to prison with hard labour for one day, and there was privately whipped with birch rods, receiving twelve strokes. He had stolen 48 farthings from Mr John Shepherd's shop in Knowsley Road.

P13-14

5. Miller's Castle, 1864.
This view of Bootle shore, by J. Beattie, shows the residence of William Miller (built 1824), the landmarks, and much seaside activity.

1865

- The foundation stone of Christ Church, C of E Church was laid on August 16th.
- A toll bar house was constructed on Stanley Road on the instructions of the Earl of Derby. The carriages from Liverpool were charged 6d and from Bootle 3d.
- The Wesleyan Church in Sheridan Place was sold to the Primitive Methodists.

1866

- The Bishop of Chester the Rt Rev. William Jacobson consecrated Christ Church, C of E Church in Breeze Hill on October 18th, the Feast of St Luke. John Philips Mather of Bootle Hall built the church at a cost of £8,000 in memory of his crippled daughter Sophia. His son the Rev. Edward Lushington Mather was installed as the first Vicar.
- Christ Church School in Park Street was opened in October with accommodation for 400 pupils. The school had three departments. The Headteachers appointed were: Mr Stephen Hale (Boys), Miss Ellen Hawthorne (Girls) and Miss Margaret Brades (Infants).
- The Bootle Choral Society was founded.
- The Sanitary Act replaced the Nuisance Act and the definition of the term 'nuisance' was extended to include overcrowding, and expanded to cover factories and workshops.
- Opening of the Molyneux Assembly Rooms in Merton Road next to Bootle Village Station.
- The Lancashire & Yorkshire Railway Company opened Ford Station in Bridle Road. A passenger service ran from Liverpool Exchange station via Bootle Junction to Ormskirk. Goods trains to Carlisle also operated on this line. The line closed in 1955.
- Valuation of Bootle-cum-Linacre for assessing the county rate was £45,254.

1867

- Opening of the Bootle - Aintree branch of the Lancashire & Yorkshire Railway.
- Linacre Gasworks was opened in Litherland Road. It was sited alongside the canal to facilitate the delivery of fuel by barge.
- St Alexander's RC Church was opened in Brasenose Road. The origin of the church dates back to 1862 when a group of Irish immigrants first met in the hayloft of a house in Derby Road. The Rev. Edward Powell was appointed Parish Priest

1868

- A Charter Party consisting William Molyneux (chairman), Samuel Baker, Joseph Musker, Robert Smith, Henry Musker, Alexander Starkey, George Ellis, John Tattersall and J.C. Cave-Browne-Cave (secretary) was formed to petition the Privy Council that a Charter of Incorporation be granted to the township of Bootle-cum-Linacre. On December 30th the Borough of Bootle was granted a Royal Charter under the Municipal Corporations Act of 1835. The Borough was divided into three wards, with a Council consisting of six aldermen and eighteen councillors.
- Joseph Gardner & Sons Ltd, timber merchants, opened premises at 123 Regent Road. The company had been founded in Liverpool in 1748.

P43-1

6. The first Mayor, Charles Howson
Bootle gained borough status in December 1868.
The first Mayor, Charles Howson (pictured) was elected in March 1869.

- Prior to incorporation the Borough was under the jurisdiction, for police purposes, of the Justices of the County of Lancaster and formed part of the West Derby Police District, a situation that continued until 1887.
- Bootle Cricket Club played the Australian Cricket XI.

7. Haymaking in Bootle
Haymaking in Bootle, 1869, with Linacre Village in the background.
These fields later became North Park.

B217

1869

- The Charter Party deputation returned in triumph from London on January 5th and was greeted by enthusiastic crowds. The Charter was carried in procession through the town and publicly read at St Mary's School. Later the Ratepayers' Association and their supporters dined together at the Dolfin Hotel in Portland Place.
- The first election of Councillors took place on March 9th.
- The first meeting of the Borough Council was held on March 16th in the Molyneux Assembly rooms. Charles Howson was elected Mayor and six aldermen were elected.
- Richard Jones, the Manager of the South Wales Bank, was appointed Borough Treasurer and on June 2nd the first Borough Rate of 7d in the £ was levied.
- A Coat of Arms was granted to the Borough on November 4th. In the same month William Geves was elected Mayor. To mark the occasion a medal was struck, bearing the Borough's coat of arms and the inscription 'William Geves unanimously elected 8th November 1869 Mayor of the Borough of Bootle-cum-Linacre'.
- The Bootle-cum-Linacre Mission congregation moved their place of worship to a cottage in Linacre Lane.
- Founding of Robert Bogle, Family Tea Dealer and Provision Merchant, at 51 Stanley Road.
- Richard Holden a solicitor was appointed Town Clerk, a post he held until 1870.
- Opening of the Castle Hotel, which took its name from the nearby Miller's Castle. The hotel stands on the corner of Regent Road and Miller's Bridge and is now known as Nina's.
- The Dee Oil Co. Ltd. established their Delta Works in Irlam Road
- Following the death of Edward Stanley, 14th Earl of Derby, the inhabitants of Bootle, as a mark of their respect and esteem erected a drinking fountain in his memory at the junction of Merton and Hawthorne Roads. The fountain was removed in 1959 when the traffic island was created. It lay forgotten for many years in Pine Grove Corporation Yard until it was erected in Southport Road opposite Hillside High School in 1989.

1870

- The Earl of Derby laid the foundation stone of Bootle Hospital on April 24th. A 'grand fancy dress fair and flower show' was held to mark the event.
- For the first time, in November, the Registrar at West Derby provided a monthly return for Bootle; it showed 69 births and 32 deaths during the month.
- Following the passing of the Elementary Education Act a School Board consisting of nine members was established on November 30th. The Board's first meeting was held on December 15th with Mr Conning as its chairman, the minutes being taken by Mr Pierce the Town Clerk.
- A branch railway line was opened from Lime Street to Bootle via Edge Hill and Walton.
- Because of an increase in traffic Coffee House Bridge was further widened to produce, between the parapets, a carriageway 33' 8" wide.
- To improve its response to fires in the town the council purchased a hand-drawn hose-reel cart.
- The Misses Donaldson ran a private school for young ladies at 9 St Catherine's Road. The syllabus included Latin, French, German, Science and Music.
- St Mary's School was enlarged to accommodate 440 pupils.
- Bootle-cum-Linacre Mission congregation moved to a small building in New Street, off Linacre Lane.
- Peter Lunt, a Netherton farmer began making soap using the blubber from a whale stranded on Crosby Beach. From this small beginning grew the company of Peter Lunt & Co. Ltd. Lunt Avenue in Netherton is named after him.
- The Health Committee informed the Lancashire & Yorkshire Railway Company of the dangers of the Marsh Lane level crossing and the need for the construction of a footbridge or subway.

- At this time there were 28 schools operating in the Borough providing education for 2,528 pupils. Three were Church of England Schools (St John's, St Mary's and Christ Church), two Roman Catholic (St James' and St Alexander's), plus an undenominational school in Linacre Village. The remaining schools were private schools known as 'Adventure Schools', catering for between 7 and 47 children each. Two schools on the Liverpool / Bootle boundary (the United Presbyterian School in Derby Road and St Paul's C of E School, North Shore) accommodated a further 150 Bootle pupils.

1871

- The census taken on March 1st showed 16,247 people living in Bootle.
- A dispensary was established at 146/148 Berry Street.
- Municipal offices were established in the Molyneux Rooms in Merton Road.
- The Canada Half-tide Basin was enlarged.
- Parents unable to pay their children's school fees could apply to the School Board for help. Applications had to be made in person and were rigorously scrutinised.
- A Welsh Baptist Chapel was erected in Brasenose Road, the congregation having previously met in Princes Terrace.
- The bells installed in Christ Church in 1866, the heaviest peal of steel bells in the country, proved too heavy for the tower. A peal that had been made for St Phillip's Church in Litherland, but found to be unsuitable there, replaced them.
- Bootle-cum-Linacre Mission acquired premises in Waterworks Street paid for by Robert James Glasgow JP.

1872

- The Earl of Derby opened Bootle Hospital in Derby Road on April 10th. The hospital, which cost £4,200 to build, was paid for by public subscription. Miss M. A. Irvine was appointed the first matron.
- The School Board appointed Mr Brumfitt as the Council's first School Board Visitor (Attendance Officer). He wore a uniform and his job included checking up on children playing truant from school, keeping a record of all children in the Borough under the age of 13 and the number of pupils who were half-timers.
- The valuation of Bootle-cum-Linacre for assessing the County rate was £68,660.
- Formation of what was to become the core of the congregation that later worshipped in Emmanuel Church. Until the church was built in Stanley Road they worshipped in the Molyneux rooms in Merton Road.
- Bootle Working Men's Conservative Association was founded.
- St James' RC School was moved to new premises in Chesnut Grove.
- The company of Wright & Hanlon, leather goods manufacturers, was founded in Bootle.
- W. Alf Ascroft opened a Land and Estate Agents and Valuer's office in Stanley Road.

8. Bootle Borough Hospital   X008605601 album
Bootle Borough Hospital, Derby Road, opened 1872 and later enlarged.

1873

- An extra wing was added to Christ Church School in Park Street and a memorial stone recording the fact reads: 'In loving memory of Robert Pendleton born 1822 died 1866 by whose munificent request to Christ Church Schools this additional wing was erected A.D. 1873'.
- Samuel Walters the marine artist built two houses in Merton Road named Staniland Villas where he lived until his death in 1882. St Winefride's RC Church now stands on the site.
- Dr R.J. Sprakeling was appointed Bootle's first Medical Officer of Health.

1874

- Christ Church Mission Church was opened in Waterworks Street in April to provide a place of worship for the poor of the parish. The Mather family, the builders of Christ Church, met the cost of the building.
- In July the residents of Breeze Hill complained to the Watch Committee that women drying cotton goods in the neighbourhood were trespassing and using obscene language.
- A new fire engine called the 'Pioneer' came into service in November.
- In December Mrs. Evans opened a Dame School for 20 pupils in Howe Street.
- The School Board office was located at 80 Merton Road.

- Opening of a Mission Hall in Sheridan Place in connection with St John's Church.
- The firm of Gilbert Norris, furniture removers, was founded in Bootle.
- William Hartley established a factory for the making of jams at 50 Pine Grove.
- J.A. Picton, after whom the Picton Library in Liverpool is named, laid the foundation stone of Emmanuel Congregational Church in Stanley Road.
- The builder William Evans built a house on the corner of Stanley and Balliol Roads that later became Connolly House. The building incorporated a variety of different building styles as an exemplar for potential customers. It was demolished in 2006.

1875

- James Blackledge, who was born in Sefton Village in 1822, opened flourmills in Derby Road. Eighty men and twelve boys were employed. This later became Blackledge's Bakery.
- The retiring Mayor, Alderman George Barnes, presented a large and a small locket to be worn by his successors. The Mayors in succeeding years each added a link until 1891, when the Council decided the chain was long and heavy enough!

1876

- Emmanuel Congregational Church at the junction of Stanley and Balliol Roads was opened on February 17th. The first minister was the Rev. George P. Jarvis; Mr J. Clarke of 27 Church View was appointed keeper of the church at a salary of £24 per annum. Vandals burnt down the church in the 1960s.
- David Philip Davies laid the foundation stone of the Welsh Calvinistic Methodist Church on the corner of Trinity and Stanley Roads on May 17th. The congregation had previously worshipped in a church on the corner of Balliol and Brasenose Roads.
- A petition was sent to Queen Victoria on September 15th requesting permission to establish a Magistrates Court in Bootle because the police had to walk their charges all the way to Basnett Street in Liverpool. Later in the year a Commission of the Peace was granted to Bootle enabling them to appoint their own Justices.
- The Bootle Times newspaper was founded on September 24th in offices at 107 Balliol Road in premises previously occupied by a Welsh Calvinistic Methodist Church.
- The 1876 Education Act required Boroughs to set up Attendance Committees, something that Bootle had already done. Children under ten were not to be employed and those between ten and fourteen could only enter employment provided they had reached a satisfactory level in reading, writing and arithmetic.
- The firm of Ed. Mills & Son, blacksmiths, was founded at 10-20 Salisbury Road.

1877

- On January 27th the following people were appointed Bootle's first Justices of the Peace: William Barlow, Thomas P. Danson, William Dent, William Geves, William Gibson, Thomas Lees, John P. McArthur, John Quinn and Charles Taylor. The Clerk to the

Magistrates was Edward Cotton. A Magistrates' Court was established in the Molyneux Rooms, Merton Road in February and daily petty sessions commenced on May 14th.

- The Mersey Docks & Harbour Board (MDHB) built a lighthouse on the sea wall at Bootle: the North Wall Lighthouse. Incorporated into the structure was a foghorn that became known as the Bootle Bull. In 1884 the sea wall became part of Hornby Dock.
- Mrs. Poulsom organised a concert in the Town Hall to raise funds for the hospital and this became an annual event.
- At this time horse-drawn vehicles transported most goods, and the men driving them were known as carters or hauliers. To reach out to these men a Gospel Mission was established in the Ebenezer Hall, Brasenose Road.
- Valuation of Bootle- cum-Linacre for assessing the County rate was £103,770.

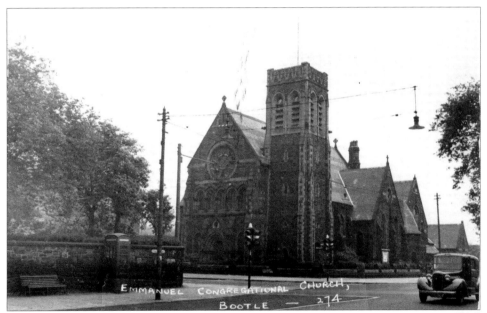

PA3-41

9. Emmanuel Congregational Church
Emmanuel Congregational Church, Stanley Road,
opened 1876, was a familiar landmark until burnt down in the 1960s.

1879

- Langton Dock and Branch Dock, named after William Langton a member of the Old Dock Committee, opened to traffic in May.
- The Earl of Derby donated to Bootle Hospital a cartload of sandstone, strips of ticking, ten hares and ten pheasants.
- James Cryer established a modern bakery and Italian warehouse at 112-114 Strand Road.

- A direction was issued by the Board of Education that people wishing to employ young people between the age of ten and fourteen must require the young person to provide a certificate of age, a certificate of school attendance and a certificate of proficiency. All these details were to be found in the child's 'School Book'.
- The 1,500 seats in St Mary's Church were occupied each Sunday.
- Bootle took up places at the Liverpool Residential Truant School in Hightown that catered for children between the ages of seven and thirteen. The cost for each child was 8/6d per week, the government contributing 3/-. The Justices could send children found playing truant from school to this and other similar institutions.
- The Bootle Temporary Relief Society was founded for the relief of the poor.
- Canada Half-tide Basin was renamed Brocklebank Dock in honour of Ralph Brocklebank, the Chairman of MDHB from 1863-69.

X008605601 album

10. Police Court
This Police Court, incorporating a Police Station, opened in Lower Strand Road in 1880.

1880

- A police court, costing £4,095 to build, was opened in Lower Strand Road on March 15th. Incorporated into the building was a police station manned by the Lancashire County police force, who were responsible for Bootle at this time.
- On April 15th Bootle, which had been part of the Anglican diocese of Chester, became part of the newly created diocese of Liverpool with the Rt. Rev. John Charles Ryle as bishop.
- The Mayor laid the foundation stone of the Town Hall on July 8th.
- Bootle children took up two-thirds of the places in St Alexander's RC School located in Liverpool.
- Bootle's first telephone exchange was established above a bakery on the corner of Princes Street and Derby Road.
- The Ormskirk, Southport and Bootle Agricultural Society show was held on the North Recreation Ground on August 8th.

1881

- The census taken on April 3rd showed 27,374 people living in Bootle.
- The Prince and Princess of Wales officially opened Langton and Alexandra Docks on September 8th. In the same month a railway link to Alexandra Dock was opened.
- Bootle residents were questioned on their views as to whether they were for or against the opening of public houses on a Sunday. The majority opposed such openings and Bootle made history by becoming the first area in England to become 'dry' on Sundays.
- The Girls' Department in St Mary's School was enlarged to cater for 72 more children.
- A very severe winter enabled people to skate on the frozen canal in Bootle. There was also a great snowstorm with drifts nine and ten feet deep in places.
- Bootle Football Club was formed.
- Bootle Corporation adopted Stanley Road and the tollgate was removed.

1882

- The Mayor opened the Town Hall and Municipal Offices in Oriel Road on Easter Monday April 10th. John Johnson designed it in the Renaissance style.
- On April 15th the Mayoress, Mrs Poulsom, was presented with an illuminated address in a casket and a dessert service in solid silver subscribed for by the inhabitants of Bootle. Messrs Tickle and Parkinson made the presentation in the Town Hall.
- The Mayor opened the first horse drawn tramway service in the Borough (Derby Road to Lime Street via Stanley Road) on July 11th.
- Samuel Walters, the marine artist, died at his home 78 Merton Road.
- The congregation of the Bootle-cum-Linacre Mission formally adopted the articles of faith and church order of the Baptist tradition.
- The Liverpool Savings Bank opened an office in St John's School in Brasenose Road.

- Beaconsfield Hall was built in Pembroke Road. The hall was built as a Conservative Club and was named after Benjamin Disraeli (Prime Minister 1874 to 1880, becoming the Earl of Beaconsfield in 1876). Lord Claude Hamilton conducted the opening ceremony.
- Everton FC played Bootle FC on their ground in Marsh Lane.
- The Bootle Institute opened at 206 Knowsley Road to provide a meeting place for working men. Over the years it became in turn a temporary school and then a cinema known as the Picture Palace.
- William Ross opened his first fruit shop in Bootle.
- The Molyneux Assembly Rooms at 80 Merton Road became a Masonic Hall.
- The Watch Committee instructed that 'On the Sabbath trams are to proceed at walking pace when passing places of worship'.

1883

- The Board of Education changed the name of the proposed Wadham Road Board School to Bedford Road Board School in February.
- During the year there were 1,440 births and 761 deaths recorded in Bootle. Of these, 407 deaths were of children under five, i.e. 53.4% of all deaths.
- A mortuary for use by Bootle Hospital was built in Nelson Street on a site leased from the L. & M. W. Railway Company. It was built as a memorial to Thomas Sands who was Lord Mayor of Liverpool 1843-44.
- In order to meet government requirements to provide sufficient day school places an attempt was made to use the Sunday School rooms at the Congregational Chapel in Trinity Road, the Welsh Presbyterian Church in Stanley Road, the Wesleyan Methodist church in Pembroke Road and the Baptist Church in Derby Road. The members of the church congregations however rejected the request
- A borough-wide survey showed that 4,445 children were attending church schools and 857 were attending private schools.
- Land for the South Recreation Ground in Balliol Road and the North Recreation Ground (formerly known as Barn Hey) in Stanley Road was acquired on a short lease from the Earl of Derby.
- Bootle Cricket Club moved to a new ground on the corner of Hawthorne and Wadham Roads.
- A Primitive Methodist Church was established at 16 Queens Road.
- Peel Road Presbyterian Church was opened.
- By the end of the year the population of Bootle had risen to 40,000.
- Thomas Draper Pierce resigned as Town Clerk following allegations that he had issued 'Fraudulent Bonds'.
- Joseph Parr Ltd, Builders' Merchants, was established on the corner of Stanley Road and Marsh Lane.
- The Muncaster Arms Hotel was built in Irlam Road.

1884

- Hornby Dock, opened in January, was named after Thomas Dyson Hornby, Chairman of the MDHB, 1876-1889.
- The North Mersey Goods Station was opened in February.
- Bootle adopted the Public Libraries Act on March 19th.
- Bootle Cricket Club's new pavilion, costing £2,000, opened in April.
- In April it was decided to open the gallery in the Council Chamber to the public during Council meetings. Admission was by ticket, with one ticket being allocated to each Council Member.
- The Bank of Liverpool opened its first Bootle branch at 325 Derby Road on May 1st (Later a branch of Martin's Bank)
- The Rt. Rev. Joseph O'Farrell, Bishop of New Jersey, USA, assisted the Roman Catholic Bishop of Liverpool when he laid the foundation stone of St James RC Church in Chesnut Grove on July 20th. Work also began on building a new St James' RC School. The total cost of the project was £25,000.
- A lamp, cattle trough and drinking fountain were erected at the junction of Rimrose and Peel Roads.
- The first edition of the Christ Church magazine 'Parish Leaves' was published.
- The valuation of Bootle-cum-Linacre for assessing the County rate was £278,692.
- Opening of the Post Office on the corner of Merton and Litherland Roads.
- Opening of Marsh Lane Station.
- A steam-driven fire engine to replace the old manual engine was purchased; it was named after Councillor Ibbs. A Merryweather fire escape was also purchased.

1885

- The North-Western Banking Company opened a new branch in Derby Road, near St Mary's Church, on May 13th.
- Bootle Liberal Association opened the Reform Club on Stanley Road on June 1st
- The Ormskirk, Southport and Bootle Agricultural Society show was held on the North Recreation Ground on August 8th.
- Bedford Road Board School, built at a cost of £13,604 with places for 1,255 pupils, opened on August 24th. The following Headteachers were appointed: Mr A. J. Miles (Senior Boys), Miss A. J. Lace (Senior Girls), Miss S. Forshaw (Juniors) and Miss Agnes Armstrong (Infants).
- Salisbury Road Board School, built at a cost of £11,814 with places for 1,385 pupils, opened on August 24th. The following Headteachers were appointed Mr S. Leigh (Senior Boys), Miss Chadwick (Senior Girls), Miss Dixon (Junior Boys), Miss Tanner (Junior Girls) and Miss H. Wharham (Infants).
- The Mayor laid the foundation stone of the Free Public Library in Oriel Road on November 4th.

11. Bedford Road Board School, built 1885.

X008605601 album

- Each year on a Sunday in late November the Mayor attended morning worship at one local church and evening worship at another. This became known as Hospital Sunday because collections taken up during the services were donated to Bootle Hospital. In 1885 the Mayor, Alderman Matthew Hill, attended St Mary's Church in the morning and Emmanuel Church in the evening.
- Children in Bootle had to pay a weekly fee to go to school: under five 1d; age 5-7 2d, standard 1, 3d; standard 2, 4d; standards 3 & 4, 5d; standards 5-7, 6d.
- Mr Brown the Headmaster of Salisbury Road School started teaching evening classes in animal physiology and physiography. The following year the curriculum was extended to include the 'precepts of agriculture and hygiene'.
- Cocoa rooms, inspired by the Temperance Movement, were opened in Strand Road.
- St Paul's Presbyterian Church was established in Peel Road.
- The Sanitary Dry Lime Co. opened their Britannia Works at 50 Brasenose Road.
- Land was purchased in Linacre Lane, Orrell, on which to build a Fever Hospital.

1886
- The R.C. Bishop of Liverpool consecrated St James' RC Church in Chesnut Grove on July 1st
- In November cookery rooms were installed in Bedford and Salisbury Road Schools.
- A Penny Bank was started in Bedford and Salisbury Road Schools.
- Bootle-cum-Linacre Mission congregation who had joined the Baptist Union in 1882 moved to newly-built premises in Ash Street.
- Beaconsfield Hall in Pembroke Road became known as County Hall.

1887
- Alderman Matthew Hill formally opened the Bootle Corporation Infectious Diseases Hospital in Linacre Lane on January 18th.
- In January the Council Chamber was reconstructed. The room was decorated and a stained glass window was installed to commemorate the Golden Jubilee of Queen Victoria.
- On February 9th a collection of minerals, fossils etc. for the Borough Museum was purchased from the Liverpool Royal Institution out of gifts by the Earl of Derby, and the trustees of the Danson Bequest
- JP Boswell erected a new circus building in February at the junction of Strand and Irlam Roads.
- The Bishop of Liverpool licensed St Matthew's C of E Church in Stanley Road on March 29th. The church at this time was a small corrugated iron hut. The first Vicar, the Rev. Arthur West Oliver, served until 1902. Like many of his fellow clergy of all denominations the vicar served on the Bootle School Board and later the Education Committee.
- The Mayor opened the Free Library, Museum and Reading Room in Oriel Road on June 22nd. This formed part of the celebration of Queen Victoria's Golden Jubilee. The library

housed a collection of 4,808 books. Dr. Tudor made a gift to the Free Library of 1,500 books from his own library on July 11th.
- A Borough Police Force was established on July 1st and Captain Arrowsmith was appointed Chief Constable, at a salary of £300 per annum. A police station was opened at 3 Derby Road, in premises rented from the police surgeon Dr. Sprakeling, at a rent of £50 per annum. The County Force continued to use the Lower Strand Road station and was responsible for policing the rural parts of the Bootle division.
- Thomas Henry Ismay, the owner of the White Star Line shipping company, opened a new wing at Bootle Hospital on August 27th.
- Charles Dickens, eldest son of the famous author, gave a reading from his father's works at County Hall, Pembroke Road, on October 14th prior to his departure for America on a lecture tour.
- Miss Gregson donated an Economic and Natural History collection to Bootle Museum in October.
- Free popular lectures arranged by the Library Committee began on November 15th
- Evening classes started in Bedford Road School on three evenings a week. Subjects included reading, arithmetic, dictation, composition, drawing, singing, musical drill, woodcarving, cookery and needlework.
- Higher Education in Bootle began with a staff of two and some twenty students meeting in the basement of the public library.
- A Borough Fire Brigade was established under Superintendent G.W. Parker. The police court and station in Lower Strand Road became the Borough's first fire station.
- A mission church in connection with Ash Street Baptist Church was established in Sussex Street.
- N. Molyneux & Sons, vehicle builders, was established at 39-43 Church View, close to Coffee House Bridge.
- The Presbyterian Church in Derby Road was closed and the congregation moved to a new, much larger building on the corner of Trinity and Hawthorne Roads. It became known as Trinity Presbyterian Church in acknowledgement of its new location.

1888
- The Bank of Liverpool opened its second Bootle branch at 211 Stanley Road on February 21st A third branch followed in March at 508 Stanley Road. (Both later became branches of Martin's Bank)
- The Mayor opened the baths and gymnasium in Balliol Road on May 7th. Built at a cost of £14,849 the building contained two plunge baths (one each for ladies and gentlemen, for swimming) and also slipper baths, where local people without bathrooms in their homes could pay a small charge and have a bath.
- School Board offices were opened on October 12th on the corner of Balliol and Kings Roads. In the 1960s the building was used as a school clinic.

- Mrs. T. W. Cookson laid the foundation stone of St Leonard's Church on October 15th.
- The old wing of the Borough Hospital was renovated.
- Two new private schools were recorded in Bootle: Bootle College at 31 Breeze Hill and a Seminary for Young Ladies at Belgravia Villa, 18 St Albans Road.
- The first police detectives were appointed to the Bootle force.
- Bootle FC beat Everton FC 2-1 in front of a crowd of 10,000 on their Marsh Lane ground.
- Opening of the new Litherland Road Bridge across the Leeds and Liverpool Canal.
- Marsh Lane Methodist Church opened a Sunday School and chapel in Cyprus Road. It was extended in 1893.
- Formation of a Ladies Committee later known as the 'Linen League' to raise funds to provide equipment for Bootle Hospital.

1889

- In January Mr W. A. Mathieson, an old Bootle resident, presented a horse-drawn ambulance to Bootle Hospital. As a result the hospital became the first public institution in the country to provide a public ambulance service. In the same month Mr Mathieson presented a mace to the Corporation.
- As a result of the Local Government Act of 1888 Bootle-cum-Linacre was created a County Borough on April 1st
- In April the Bank of Liverpool opened its fourth Bootle branch at 99 Stanley Road (later Martin's Bank)
- The foundation stone of a new Balliol Road Methodist Church and Sunday School on the corner of Pembroke and Balliol Roads was laid on May 21st The Sunday School was capable of accommodating 600 pupils. The original church had been opened on the site in 1865.
- A 'birching block' was purchased in August to ensure that boys, when birched, could be held secure so that their spines were not damaged. It was reported that more boys were birched in Bootle during the year than in the whole of the Liverpool district.
- The Bishop of Liverpool consecrated St Leonard's C of E Church in Peel Road on St Leonard's Day November 6th. The church, designed by George Bradbury was built on land given by the Earl of Derby. The first incumbent was the Rev. James Denton Thompson.
- The Mayor inaugurated the distribution of Christmas hot pots for the deserving poor in December.
- The two Board Schools, Bedford and Salisbury, were inspected by representatives from the Board of Education in London. Over 95% of the pupils reached the required level in reading, writing and arithmetic. The outcome of the tests dictated the level of grant allocated to the local Board by central government.
- The Bootle branch of the National Union of Dock Labourers was established.
- Cartlands Circus from the USA was held on a site at the junction of Strand and Irlam Roads. It included Wild West scenes involving William Cody, otherwise known as 'Buffalo Bill'.

1890

- Due to overcrowding, all pupils attending Bedford Road School who lived in Liverpool were required to leave in January.
- A dock strike started on March 3rd affecting the Bootle docks. The strike lasted until April 4th, during which time the army was on standby.
- The R.C. Bishop of Liverpool dedicated a new altar and sanctuary in St James RC Church in May.
- The Mayor laid the foundation stone of the new police buildings in Oriel Road on June 23rd. In the cavity of the cornerstone were placed a bottle containing copies of the Bootle Times and other local papers; coins i.e. a crown piece, double florin, half-a-crown, shilling, sixpence, threepenny bit, penny, halfpenny, farthing; plus a copy of the Corporation Yearbook for 1890.
- On August 14th the Royal Assent was given to the Bootle Corporation Act, by which the borough boundaries were amended. This changed the name from Bootle-cum-Linacre to Bootle. The Council was increased from three to five wards, each returning six councillors. In addition the number of aldermen was increased from six to ten.
- The Royal Muncaster Theatre in Irlam Road, also known as the New Prince's Theatre, was opened on October 6th. The Pennington family who hailed from Muncaster Castle in Cumberland owned the theatre.
- The Earl of Lathom laid the foundation stone of St Matthew's C of E Church in Stanley Road on October 9th. The Earl of Derby gave the site for the church; the cost of the building was £5,500.
- In October Bootle's Chief Constable advertised for police constables in the Dumfries and Perth newspapers in Scotland with a view to getting 'a better class of men'.
- The first election of councillors to the new wards, Linacre and Mersey, was held on November 1st. The election of four additional aldermen to complete the enlarged Council took place on November 9th.
- The Bootle Cycling Club was established.
- George H. Poole and Sons established a factory in Canal Street to refine borax.
- The Unitarian Church in Stanley Road, capable of accommodating 200 worshippers, was opened.

1891

- The census taken on April 5th showed 49,217 people living in Bootle.
- In August the children's section of the Free Library was opened.
- Bootle adopted the Elementary Education Act, sometimes known as the 'Free Education Act', on September 1st. Government grants were paid to local Boards of Education who became responsible for providing free elementary education for all children.
- A Technical School was established in the basement of the Free Library in Oriel Road on September 28th. The first Principal was Mr J.J. Ogle who was also the Chief Librarian.

- The Mayor opened the new Police Station and Magistrates Court in Oriel Road on October 22nd. The bench consisted of 37 justices and the police force numbered 76. It was built at a cost of £13,096.
- The Bishop of Liverpool consecrated St Matthew's C of E Church in Stanley Road on December 5th.
- The gates of local schools were locked at 9.15 a.m. and again at 1.45 p.m. after which times the children were regarded as being late. Children who were late were often caned.
- The Primitive Methodist Church in Queens Road was re-opened.
- The Rt. Rev. Dr. Bardsley Bishop of Sodor and Man, opened the new Parochial Hall and Sunday School at St Leonard's Church.
- The Earl of Derby donated the land for what was to become Derby Park. Contemporary records refer to it both as 'Bootle Park' and 'New Park'.
- The firm of Harrison Ltd., Woodturners, was founded in Hemans Street.

1892
- On May 17th the Mayor held a reception for the delegates to the General Assembly of the Welsh Presbyterians who were holding their Annual General Meeting in Bootle.
- Mr T.E. Blundell was given the contract for winding and repairing the fifteen clocks in the Board's schools and offices at a cost of £5 per annum.
- As the result of a significant increase in pupil numbers the Board of Education rented the Bootle Institute in Knowsley Road in which to set up a temporary school.
- The Primitive Methodist Church in Sheridan Place was bought by the Wesleyan Methodists and named Wesley Hall.

1893
- The Liverpool Overhead Railway extension to Alexandra Dock was opened on March 6th.
- A cyclists and harriers carnival, organised by the Licensed Victualler's Cycling Club, was held on June 19th.
- On November 7th the Mayor chaired a meeting in the Town Hall to arrange an extension into Bootle of the work of the Society for the Prevention of Cruelty to Children.
- The Earl of Derby distributed prizes to the students of the Bootle Corporation Technical Schools on December 19th
- Mrs. Poulsom received an illuminated address in a silver casket, a diamond bracelet, a silver salver and a silver bowl marking her charitable work over a period of 16 years, particularly in connection with Bootle Hospital.
- The Board of Education Inspectors in London complained that Salisbury Road School was overcrowded. In consequence the Bootle School Board decided that all pupils attending Bootle schools who did not live within the Borough must leave before the Government's next annual inspection.

- Blackledge's new bakery was built in Derby Road.
- A tramway to Litherland was constructed along Stanley and Linacre Roads.
- The first ball to raise funds for Bootle Hospital was hosted by the Mayor in the Town Hall. This was to become an annual event that featured high on the social calendar and raised substantial sums of money for the hospital.
- The firm of A. Atkins & Sons, transport contractors, was established in Langdale Street.

1894
- In January Nurse Lincoln was appointed to Christ Church as parish nurse to give advice and support to the poor of the parish.
- The Earl of Derby was the guest of honour at a reception and banquet held in Bootle Town Hall on March 20th, hosted by the Mayor, Alderman B. S. Johnson.
- A refuse destructor and sanitary wharf were opened in Pine Grove on April 11th.
- On April 19th a decision was taken to create an Industrial School in Bootle. A site was chosen on the corner of Marsh Lane and Irlam Road where a former convent was converted for school use. This was to provide schooling for the 'helpless children of grossly neglectful, criminal and immoral parents'. Until the creation of the school, Bootle had paid for these children to be educated in Industrial schools outside the Borough.
- The Lord Mayor of Liverpool, Alderman W.B. Bowring, laid the foundation stone of the Unitarian Free Church in Stanley Road in July. The church was sited between Trinity Road and what was to become Morton Gardens.
- The Liverpool Overhead Railway Company opened a new station at Langton Dock in August
- A Sale of Work was held in the Town Hall on November 2nd in aid of the Bootle Shelter for the Prevention of Cruelty to Children.
- The first School Library Service in the country commenced in Bootle in December. It was the suggestion of Mr A.J. Miles, the Headmaster of Bedford Road Board School, whose school was first to benefit from the service.
- A decision was taken by the Council that occupiers of property abutting on to any pavement were required to move snow that fell on it as soon as convenient after the end of the fall.
- A decision was taken by the School Board that female teachers who became pregnant had to cease to work for the Board at least five months before their confinement. A subsequent decision later in the year decreed that all female teachers must resign when they married.
- The firm of George Parr Ltd. was founded in premises in Stanley Road and became famous for 'Aunt Sally' liquid soap.
- The Bootle Photographic Society was founded and held its first exhibition.
- Orrell Parish Council was established.

1895

- Hawthorne Road Board School to accommodate 957 pupils was opened on March 11th by Dr. Canavan, Chairman of the School Board. The Headteachers appointed were Mr J.H.J. Stringer (Boys), Miss Taylor (Girls) and Miss E. Forshaw (Infants).
- Derby Park, 22 acres in extent, opened to the public on August 17th.
- The Day Industrial School in Marsh Lane was opened on December 2nd catering for 300 pupils. The Superintendent was Miss P. Wall. Day Industrial Schools operated under Home Office regulations.

12. Derby Park   X008605601 album
Derby Park, opened 1895. A few years later, this Edwardian garden party scene still shows open countryside to the north.

1896

- In January the foundation stone of Stanley Road Baptist Church was laid: the church opened for worship in September. The congregation had previously met in a chapel on the corner of Derby Road and Chapel Street.
- Bootle's first 'May Day' celebrations were held in North Park on May 2nd when Miss Alice Parry was crowned May Queen. The event, which was initially set up to raise funds

for Bootle Hospital, became an annual event and continued, apart from the war years, until 1940. After the Second World War it became the Bootle Carnival and was held in Bootle Stadium. The last carnival was in 1966.
- The Annual Conference of the Wesleyan Methodist Church was held in Bootle on July 30th.
- The Countess of Derby opened the Liverpool and Bootle Police Orphanage at Sunnyside in Woolton on October 6th.
- A public gymnasium was opened on November 4th in the gentleman's swimming baths.
- Formation of the Liverpool North-end and District Scottish Association, known as the 'Bootle Scottish'. Meetings were held in the old Masonic Hall in Merton Road.
- Work was completed on the building of the tower of St James' RC Church.
- Work commenced on St Paul's Presbyterian Church in Peel Road to enlarge it to provide room for a congregation of 600. The work was not completed until 1902.
- The members of Emmanuel Congregational Church opened a mission hall in Marsh Street.
- The foundations were laid for a new factory for Johnson's Cleaners & Dyers in Mildmay Road.
- The firm of Burley & Sons Ltd., handlemakers and wood turners, was established in Hornby Road.
- A branch dock was added to Canada Dock.
- Opening of St Winefride's RC Church on the corner of Derby Road and Chapel Street in a building previously used as a Baptist Chapel. The first Parish Priest was the Rev. Henry Blanchard.
- The Penpoll Works of Campbell & Isherwood was established in Hawthorne Road for the manufacture of electrical goods.

1897

- Queen Victoria's Diamond Jubilee was celebrated during the week commencing June 20th. Schoolchildren received medals to commemorate the occasion and the Mayor held a reception for old people in the Town Hall. There was music performed in Derby Park and the North and South Recreation Grounds by the Borough Band, St Luke's Band and the Kirkdale Industrial School Band. On the evening of June 22nd there was a firework display in the North Recreation Ground. The week's festivities raised £3,000 for Bootle Hospital.
- Morton Gardens on Stanley Road opened on July 31st. The gardens were named after Alderman Andrew Morton, Chairman of the Parks & Baths Committee. The gardens closed in 1960 when the Stanley Precinct was built.
- Liverpool United Tramways & Omnibus Company acquired Bootle's tramway system in September.
- A clock that chimed the hours was installed in the tower of Christ Church to mark Queen Victoria's Diamond Jubilee. The clock was lit by gas.
- Opening of Marsh Lane Welsh Congregational Church seating 500.

1898

- On April 13th the North and South Wales Bank Ltd opened a branch at 185 Stanley Road. The bank started its life in the Reform Club housed in Stanley Hall.
- Johnson's Cleaners & Dyers became a limited company.
- School Library Service deliveries started to Hawthorne Road School.
- The Sanitary Paint Co, Ltd opened premises in Rimrose Road.
- A Welsh Baptist Chapel was opened in Balliol Road seating 450. The congregation had previously worshipped in a chapel in Brasenose Road.

1899

- The Mayor opened an electricity generating station in Pine Grove on April 20th.
- Knowsley Road temporary school was closed in July and Gray Street Board School for 974 pupils was opened on August 14th. The Headteachers appointed were Mr W Milroy (Boys), Miss Tatton (Girls) and Miss Paterson (Infants).
- A decision was taken to pay schoolteachers who held university degrees an extra £5 per annum.
- A mission room was established in a room above a shop in Hawthorne Road between Province and Aughton Roads. This was later to develop into the parish of St John & St James.
- The Bootle Irish National Club was established in Derby Road.
- The North and South Wales Bank Ltd, later to become the Midland Bank and subsequently HSBC, moved to 197 Stanley Road on which site it remains to this day.
- Opening of the Welsh Congregational Church in Trinity Road, with seating for 400.

1900

- An electric tramway service began on May 27th, serving the Rimrose Road, Knowsley Road and Stanley Road routes. Services to the Derby Road area were introduced on December 9th. The trams were known as 'toast racks' because the upper deck was open and the rows of seats resembled a toast rack.
- From July 4th Bedford Road School was declared a 'free school'. This meant that parents no longer had to make a contribution for their children's education.
- On July 5th a Flower Show was held in Derby Park.
- The first meeting of the Orrell branch of the Presbyterian Church was held at 5 Monfa Road in July with eight people in attendance. The congregation soon grew and in 1902 built a church in Springwell Road on land given by William Jones, the local builder.
- The Earl of Derby opened the Bootle Technical School in Balliol Road on September 27th: Mr J.J. Ogle was appointed Principal. The school had started as a technical instruction centre operating in the basement of the library in Oriel Road.
- A Röntgen X-ray apparatus was purchased for use in Bootle hospital.
- The Bootle School of Art opened in buildings in Stanley Road and Hubert Bulmer was appointed Headmaster.

- A tin hut, known locally as the 'iron church' was erected in Hawthorne Road, Orrell, as a Chapel of Ease to St Phillip's C of E Church, Litherland. The Rev Colin Dawson was placed in charge as Curate.
- Opening of a Gospel Hall in Stanley Road. This later became the Sun Hall Picture House.
- School Library Service deliveries started to Salisbury Road School.
- Thomas Henry Ismay the shipping owner left £1,000 to Bootle Hospital. A ward for children was named in his memory.
- The Bootle Tanning Company opened in Well Lane.
- Blacks Ltd., manufacturer of tin boxes, was founded at 70 Litherland Road.

B1385

13. Salisbury Road Board School
Salisbury Road Board School: senior girls, pictured about 1900. The school was built in 1885.

1901

- The Mayor opened the Municipal Intermediate Day School, later the Secondary School for Boys, in the Technical School premises in Balliol Road. It was for boys from twelve years of age, who took a three-year course. Mr F. Gorse was appointed Headmaster.
- On January 28th the Mayor made a public proclamation from the steps of the Town Hall to announce the accession of King Edward VII.
- A special memorial service for Queen Victoria was held in St Mary's Church on February 3rd.

X008605601 album

14. Balliol Road Gardens

Balliol Road Gardens, opened 1901. The Baths can be seen on the left. In 1910 the Girls' Secondary School was opened on the garden site; in the 1990s Hugh Baird College built a new campus on the site.

- The census taken on March 31st showed 58,556 people living in Bootle.
- St Andrew's C of E Church opened in temporary buildings in April.
- On June 29th the Strand Road line of the electric tramway service started.
- The Mayor opened Balliol Gardens on July 9th.
- Following an outbreak of scarlatina, Bootle Hospital was closed while the building was decorated internally and externally. Electric lighting was also installed at this time.
- Three extra classrooms were added to Bedford Road Board School to cope with rising numbers.
- Electric street lighting was extended to Gray Street and Akenside Street.
- The first motorcar was sighted in Bootle.
- The Bootle Concertina Band was formed at a meeting in Marsh Lane.
- Arrest of Thomas Goudie, employee of the Bank of Liverpool, who had embezzled £170,000 to pay off gambling debts and then hidden for months in Berry Street, yards from the Oriel Road police station. The arrest was restaged just days later by Lancashire film pioneers Sagar Mitchell and James Kenyon – probably the first-ever crime reconstruction on moving film.

1902

- There was a programme of festivities during June to celebrate the coronation of King Edward VII. On June 26th all the schoolchildren assembled in the North Recreation Ground where loyal anthems were sung. The children then returned to their schools where each child received a souvenir cup and medal. (These festivities had originally been planned to coincide with the King's Coronation on June 26th but the King required an appendicitis operation so the Coronation was moved to August 9th).
- The Mayor laid the foundation stone of the new Central Fire Station, firemen's dwellings and police sub-station in Strand Road on June 27th.
- The Mayor officially opened Marsh Lane Open-air Baths, Library and Assembly Rooms on June 27th.
- On June 28th the Mayor and Mayoress gave a dinner in the Town Hall for elderly people as part of the coronation celebrations.
- The Presbyterian Church in Springwell Road was officially opened in July.
- Electric lighting was installed in Bedford Road Board School.
- The Earl of Derby extended the leases for the North and South Recreation Grounds to 999 years.
- St James' Select School was opened to cater for Roman Catholic children from Bootle who came from the more affluent families. The Headteachers appointed were Mr J. T. Hogan (Boys' and Girls' department) and Miss T. Crean (Infants).
- Founding of the Bootle District Nursing Association.
- Arthur Short was the first Labour Councillor to be elected in Bootle. He represented Linacre Ward.

- The Rev. Charles Lester, Vicar of St John's C of E Church, gave permission for a public garden to be created in the churchyard.

X008605601 album

15. Bootle Cricket Club ground
Bootle Cricket Club ground, 1903. The club was founded in 1833 and moved to this Hawthorne Road site in 1883.

1903

- On January 8th the Mayor and his wife held a Juvenile Ball for the children of Bootle aged between 5 and 15. Attendance was by invitation; as well as dancing there were marionettes, a Punch and Judy show and refreshments. This was an annual event for which decorative tickets were issued, a collection of which is preserved by Sefton Library Service.
- A street demonstration in the form of a march was held on January 10th to protest against the predatory wish of Liverpool to absorb Bootle within its boundaries.
- The Countess of Sefton laid the foundation stone of St Andrew's C of E Church on May 16th.
- Bootle School Board was abolished in May and its duties were taken over by an Education Committee appointed under the Education Act 1902. Board Schools became known as

Council Schools. The first meeting of the Education Committee took place on May 28th.

- The Liverpool Corporation Bill for the annexation of Bootle was rejected by Parliament in July. The Mayor, Alderman Sir William Clemmey, sent a telegram from the House of Commons that read 'Thank God we've won'.
- The Bootle Division of the St John Ambulance Brigade was founded on October 3rd.
- A fee-paying preparatory school, from which pupils moved on to the Boys' Day Intermediate School, was opened on the corner of Balliol and Pembroke Roads.
- St Winefride's RC School was opened. The Headteachers appointed were Mr P. O'Brien (Boys), Mrs. Kearney (Girls) and Miss Noble (Infants).
- Gray Street School and some of the voluntary schools received their first books from the School Library Service.
- Merton Road Welsh Congregational Church was opened with seating for 550 worshippers.
- Lamb Brothers Ltd. established a sawmill in Derby Road.
- Spencer's Direct Supply Co., mineral water manufacturers, opened premises at 266 Stanley Road.
- A collection was taken up to pay for one or more nurses to care for the sick of Bootle in their own homes.
- Chadburns, marine instrument manufacturers, was established in Cyprus Road.
- Sussex Street Mission, an offshoot of Ash Street Baptist Church, was established in a stable loft in Sussex Street. It continued to function until 1921.

1904

- The Mayor presided at the opening of St John's parish hall in Exeter Road on February 18th.
- On April 6th Bootle adopted the Museums and Gymnasiums Act 1891 so far as it related to Museums.
- On April 13th the Mayor opened the new Central Fire Station, Strand Road, built at a cost of £32,000. It comprised an engine house with room for four steam fire engines, two horse-drawn hose tenders and an ambulance; a workshop and stabling for ten horses; plus residential accommodation for 20 married and ten single men. It was built on the site of Cartland's Circus.
- The Lancashire & Yorkshire Railway commenced their electric train service to Southport in April.
- A garden party was held in Derby Park on July 14th at which a string orchestra and the Borough Police Band provided the music; races for model yachts took place on the lake.
- The Earl and Countess of Derby opened Stanley Gardens on July 18th. The Countess also unveiled a statue of King Edward VII, the gift of Colonel Sandys the local MP. Stables for horses that pulled local trams had previously occupied the site.
- The Bishop of Liverpool consecrated St Andrew's C of E Church on November 29th. The Rev. George Jackson was inducted as the parish's first incumbent.

- A Wesleyan Chapel was opened in Marsh Lane to replace a temporary chapel in Cyprus Road.
- The London & North-Western Railway Company bought the old fire station and police courts in Lower Strand Road.
- Bootle Corporation installed a public clock in the tower of St Leonard's C of E Church.

1905

- Linacre Council School for 975 pupils was opened in Thornton Road in February. This was the first school to be built by the Council since it took over responsibility for education in the Borough from the Bootle School Board in 1903. The Headteachers appointed were Mr A Yates (Boys), Miss Gertrude Harrison (Girls) and Miss F. Deyes (Infants). In March the school received its first delivery of books from the School Library Service.
- On June 27th the death occurred, at the age of 83, of Monsignor James Nugent the Roman Catholic priest who devoted his life to the care of poor children on Merseyside. He was buried in Ford Cemetery. The public subscribed to a memorial which was erected over his grave. The memorial took the form of a statue of St Vincent de Paul succouring little children who are grouped around him. Later a statue was also erected in St John's Gardens in Liverpool.
- The Bootle Corporation Act was given the Royal Assent on August 4th. This extended the boundaries of the Borough to include the township of Orrell. The number of wards was increased to six, the number of councillors to 33 and aldermen to 11. The first elections for the new ward were held on November 1st for councillors and the 9th for aldermen.
- The Central Post Office, previously in Browne Street, was relocated to the corner of Oriel and Balliol Roads on October 1st.
- Headteachers agreed to supervise the feeding of hungry scholars during the winter period.
- The Liverpool Savings Bank opened a branch on the corner of Linacre Lane and Stanley Road.
- Founding of Bank Hall Mission in a building known as the Bankhall Girls' Institute in Stanley Road, Liverpool. The founders were Tom Belcher a local businessman and Mr F.T. Smith.
- Williams's confectioners moved their toffee works from Wood Street, Liverpool, to Waterworks Street, Bootle.
- Death of 'Big Mick' the horse who drew the last horse-drawn ambulance. The fire brigade's blacksmith had one of Mick's hooves encased and preserved as a memorial.

1906

- A new bridge over the canal in Linacre Lane was completed on February 28th.
- A memorial to the late Alderman and Mrs. William Poulsom was unveiled in Derby Park on October 25th, by the Mayor. This is the only public sculpture to a private person in Bootle.
- Miss G. Smith was appointed as the town's first Health Visitor. Her duties included giving

advice to mothers on nutrition, nursing and the isolation of children suffering from infectious diseases.

- The Nursing Division of the Bootle branch of the St John Ambulance Brigade was established.
- A Pre-Apprentice Day School was set up. There were three teachers including the Headmaster, Mr McMillan, and twenty pupils. The school was based in the Technical College building and operated for 26 hours each week, including 6-8 hours in evening classes.
- Notices were issued by the Highways Committee warning the public against the practice of throwing orange peel on the footpaths.
- Mr George Prince opened the first cinema in Bootle in a former Gospel Hall at 237 Stanley Road. It was known as the Sun Hall Cinema and could seat 785 patrons.

1907

- In May there were 266 boys on the roll of the Intermediate Day School: 30 of them had won scholarships from local Elementary Schools.
- On October 7th the Crippled Girls' Artificial Floral Exhibition was held in the Reform Club, Stanley Road.
- The Waterloo Division of the Red Cross presented Bootle Hospital with a motor ambulance. The hospital committee minutes record "The new ambulance elicits admiration as it moves swiftly through our roads with burdens of suffering from the docks, warehouses etc., to a place of succour."
- Moves were afoot to build partitions in most of the Council and Voluntary schools to divide them up into separate classrooms. The idea originated in St Mary's National School.
- Joseph Gardner & Sons Ltd., timber merchants, opened offices in Peel Road.
- Founding of the Bootle Health Society that provided health care for the poor. The society flourished until 1929 when the local authority took over its functions.

1908

- Thomas Davies gave to Bootle Museum a collection of Egyptian antiquities collected by the late Mrs. G. W. Goodison.
- The Mayor opened Peel Road children's playground on June 3rd.
- Bootle paid for 'mentally defective' children to attend Orwell Road School in Kirkdale. The children were transported to and from school by the fire brigade.
- St Matthew's church hall complex, used as a temporary elementary school for two years, catered for 200 children (infants and junior girls). This was the result of overcrowding in the local schools, a situation that was not resolved until Orrell School was opened in 1910.
- A tower was added to Emmanuel Congregational Church in Stanley Road.
- The Bootle Times newspaper opened offices in Oriel Road by the railway station.
- Bootle Institute in Knowsley Road was converted to a cinema and was known as The Picture Palace of Bootle.

B1361

16. Linacre Council School
Linacre Council School, Thornton Road, opened 1905.
This shows the book delivery service to schools (operated by Bootle Library) in action.

1909

- Following its adoption of the Feeding of Hungry Schoolchildren and the Education (Provision of Meals) Act in 1906, Bootle commenced its School Meals Service in January by forming a Schools' Canteen Committee. The committee provided clogs and breakfasts to 'necessitous children': the breakfasts were prepared on the ground floor of the Day Industrial School.
- In July, 15 free places in the Boys' Intermediate Day School were offered to boys attending local elementary schools who reached the required standard. In the event 50 boys qualified – but only 15 were admitted.
- The Bootle Roller Rink and public hall on the corner of Malvern and Stanley Roads was opened in December.
- Opening of a new building to house the manually operated telephone exchange in Exeter Road.
- A Wesleyan Methodist Reading Room was opened in Anglesey Street.
- The Olivet Christian Mission Hall was opened in Marsh Lane.
- A Unitarian Mission Hall was opened in Waterworks Street.
- Beaconsfield Hall in Pembroke Road was converted into The Winter Gardens Theatre with seating for 490 patrons.

17. Isabella Rose PA5-1
Isabella Rose was the 1909 May Queen. Here she and her retainers are with Mayor George Randall.

- John Davies Insulating Co. Ltd was established in Well Lane.
- Robinson and Co. Ltd., ships' telegraph manufacturers, founded in Liverpool in 1760, moved their business to new premises at 1-3 Knowsley Road.

1910

- The foundation stone of St John & St James C of E Church in Monfa Road was laid on April 30th.
- Orrell Council School for 1,020 pupils opened in Aughton Road on September 5th. The Headteachers appointed were Mr Alfred Philipson (Boys), Miss Mary Dixon (Girls) and Miss Margaret E. Swift (Infants).
- Sir Benjamin Johnson of Johnson's Cleaners and Dyers, who had been knighted earlier in the year, opened Bootle Secondary School for Girls in Balliol Road on September 13th. The charges for pupils were £2 per term for the children of Bootle ratepayers and £2 7/- for others. The first Headmistress was Miss Lydia Taylor. The Council agreed that refreshments costing no more than £20 were to be provided.
- Christ Church parish hall was erected in Breeze Hill. It was a two-storey building comprising ballroom, concert hall complete with stage, kitchens and dining area, and various meeting rooms. The deeds forbade the playing of cards, betting or gambling.
- The Countess of Sefton opened St Andrew's church hall in St Andrews Road.

1911

- The Mayor, before an audience of 2,000, opened the Metropole Theatre in Stanley Road on February 20th. The first production was 'Little Red Riding Hood'.
- The Bishop of Liverpool consecrated St John & St James C of E Church in Monfa Road on May 1st. Miss Wilcox erected it as a memorial to her brothers Sir John and Mr James Wilcox. The first incumbent was the Rev. Colin Dawson.
- The census taken on May 25th showed 69,876 people living in Bootle. In the election held in the same year only 8,713 were eligible to vote.
- Celebrations to mark the Coronation of King George V were held in June. On the morning of June 20th there was a presentation of souvenirs in the form of medals, books, chocolates, pipes and tobacco to 150 patients and staff at Bootle Hospital. In the afternoon there was a garden party in Derby Park.
- The Coronation celebrations continued on June 21st when medals and illustrated souvenirs were presented to the Borough's schoolchildren. This was followed on the 22nd (the actual day of the Coronation) by a band concert in front of the Town Hall, after which there was a procession round the Borough and displays in the parks. The day concluded with a firework display in the North Recreation Ground.
- Founding of the 4th Liverpool (Bootle Section) Boy Scout troop at Bootle Secondary School for Boys. The troop met each Thursday with Mr E. Beer, a teacher at the school, as Scoutmaster. This was the first Scout troop to be formed in the Borough and was later renamed the 1st Bootle troop.

- The 40th anniversary of Bootle Hospital was marked by celebrations including an address by Alderman James Webster (Mayor of Bootle 1882-84). The hospital building was extended as a memorial to King Edward VII who had died the previous year.
- The Roman Catholic Archdiocese of Liverpool was established and Bishop Thomas Whiteside was consecrated as the first Archbishop.
- Stamina Foods Ltd., manufacturers of dog biscuits and poultry food, was established in Princes Street. This was a subsidiary of Blackledge's Bakery and was used to recycle waste products from the bakery.
- The Winter Gardens Theatre in Pembroke Road changed its name to the Apollo Theatre.
- The gas lighting in Christ Church parish church was replaced by electric lighting.
- School Library Service deliveries to Orrell Council School commenced.

1912

- The Mayor opened the Borough Cemetery on January 1st; the Bishop of Liverpool consecrated the C of E section.
- A memorial service for those who died on the steamship 'Titanic' was held at St Mary's Church on April 28th.
- The Picture House on the corner of Stanley and Malvern Roads opened in July. Originally a roller skating rink, it had seating for 1,200 patrons.
- A promenade concert was held in Derby Park on July 4th. There was a display of daylight fireworks, lawn tennis and bowling competitions and model yacht racing. Howard Stephen's Concert Party provided entertainment and there was dancing to the Merton Silver Band.
- The Royal Muncaster Theatre was sold to George Prince who re-opened it on August 19th as a cinema, changing the name to the New Prince's Theatre. The first film to be shown was 'A Victim of the Mormons'.
- The Mayor opened the Palace Cinema in Marsh Lane on October 19th. It was the first purpose-built cinema in Bootle, and had seating for 1,000 patrons.
- A decision was taken to create a playing field for the secondary schools on part of the land set aside for Bootle Cemetery.
- Harland and Wolff, shipbuilders, opened large premises between Regent and Derby Roads on land previously occupied by slum property.
- Sayer's confectioners and caterers opened premises at 9 Aintree Road.
- The Liverpool Electric Cable Co. Ltd opened new premises in Linacre Lane.
- The United Kingdom Metallic Packing Syndicate Ltd. opened new premises in Bootle.
- The Bootle Picture Palace in Knowsley Road was renamed the Empire Picture Palace.

1913

- Miss Nichol was appointed as the first School Nurse on January 1st.
- The Mayor commissioned the electricity supply works in Marsh Lane on June 25th.

- King George V and Queen Mary, with their son Prince Albert, visited Bootle on July 11th to open the graving dock, the first part of Gladstone Dock. The dock was named after Robert Gladstone, second cousin of the former Prime Minister William Ewart Gladstone. The visit concluded with a dinner in the Town Hall. Local schoolchildren each received a bronze medal to commemorate the event.
- A tuberculosis dispensary was opened in Irlam Road.
- The captain and his crew of ten men were drowned when the Dock Board Hopper 'H' sank in Hornby Dock.
- The Trade Preparatory School (previously the Pre-Apprentice Day School) that was at this time operating in the old School Board offices on the corner of Balliol and Kings Roads became recognised as a Junior Technical School and in consequence attracted a larger Government grant. At this time Mr R. McMillan was in charge of the school. The following January the school moved into premises in Irlam Road previously occupied by the Day Industrial School.
- The Aerowater Direct Supply Co. Ltd., purveyor of mineral waters, was founded in Antonio Street.

1914

- The Mayor formally opened Balliol Road Council School on January 9th. The school provided places for 1,000 pupils. The Headteachers appointed were Mr W.F. Townrow (Senior Boys), Miss A. Peake (Senior Girls) and Miss Eleanor Kay (Juniors and Infants).
- In January 'Homefield', 17 Breeze Hill, the home of a Mr Glasgow, was requisitioned for use as a military hospital for the duration of the war. The superintendent was Mrs Annie McNaught.
- Founding of the 101st Liverpool (St Thomas Royden's Own) Boy Scout troop at St Mary's Church. The troop met on Tuesday and Thursday evenings in the church hall with Mr Albert Mills as Scoutmaster. (Many years later Mr Mills became Headmaster of Balliol Boys' Secondary School and Warden of Tawd Vale Scout camping ground.)
- The colours of the 7th (Bootle) Battalion, the King's (Liverpool) Regiment were deposited with the Mayor for safe keeping on August 15th, for the duration of hostilities.
- In September the military authorities requisitioned the recently opened Balliol Council School buildings to billet soldiers. The children were dispersed, some going to Christ Church parish hall in Breeze Hill and the remainder to the hall of the Presbyterian Church in Hawthorne Road.
- On December 14th recruiting meetings for the armed forces were held in the Town Hall and at the Metropole Theatre. The speakers, urging the young men of the area to 'join the colours', were the Earl of Derby, A. Bonar Law MP, T. P. O'Connor MP, Stephen Walsh MP, and Sir Benjamin Johnson.
- The Mayor opened Derby Road Pleasure Ground on December 16th.
- Bootle Hospital was renamed Bootle Borough Hospital, and King George V became its patron.

- Founding of the 18th Bootle Boy Scout troop in Orrell Council School.
- Bootle Council opened a sanatorium in Maghull.
- To cater for increasing pupil numbers an extension was built at Gray Street Council School.
- Charles E. McNabb was appointed as the first School Dentist and was provided with premises in the basement of the Town Hall.
- The first permanent Infant Welfare Clinic in Bootle was established in rented rooms in the Masonic Hall in Balliol Road.
- The Apollo Theatre in Pembroke Road was converted into a cinema.

1915

- In March the military authorities requisitioned the Day Industrial School premises. The school was moved into the Technical School buildings in Balliol Road / Pembroke Road where it remained for the duration of the war.
- In early June Christ Church parish hall was requisitioned for use as a military hospital. The first casualties from France arrived later the same month.
- In May a relief fund was set up for the victims of the 'Lusitania' disaster.
- Orrell Public Pleasure Ground was opened on June 5th when a cricket match was played between an eleven from the Boys' Secondary School and a team captained by Ted Johnson of Bootle Cricket Club, one of the best batsmen who ever played for Bootle. The facility was mainly for the use of the Boys' Secondary School but pupils from the Girls' School could use the field on Tuesday afternoons when they were provided with a one-way railway ticket.
- The Mayor opened Bootle Cemetery Chapel in June. The chapel, built in the Gothic style, can seat 100 and cost £2,000 to build.
- The military authorities vacated Balliol Council School in September and the children were able to return.
- In December Orrell Boys' Department was closed for the day to enable the members of the school's Scout troop to attend an inspection in Liverpool.
- The first motorised fire engine was purchased and named 'Ascroft' after Alderman Peter Ascroft.
- A nurses' home attached to Bootle Borough Hospital was built in Falkner Crescent, Derby Road, as a memorial to King Edward VII. The building cost (£6,000) was met by public subscription and the Bootle May Day Demonstration Committee raised the necessary funds to furnish the home. Owing to the war there was no official opening.
- A collection was made in the Borough's schools towards the purchase of a war ambulance.
- The Bishop of Liverpool opened 'Red House', a hostel for discharged prisoners, in Strand Road.

1916

- 7th-13th May was designated 'Bootle Roll of Honour' week. Residents were encouraged to patronise shops displaying posters to indicate they were taking part in the scheme: shopkeepers pledged to donate 2.5% of the week's 'takings' to a special fund. The fund was to be used (a) to supplement government pensions to widows, orphans and dependants of Liverpool and Bootle men who fell during the war and (b) to provide allowances for deserving Liverpool and Bootle cases where pensions had been refused. Not surprisingly, most shopkeepers took part.
- The Bootle School of Art in Stanley Road closed on July 31st and the School Medical Services took over the premises.
- King George V presented local hero Private Arthur Herbert Procter of the 1/5 Battalion, King's (Liverpool) Regiment with the Victoria Cross, for action he took at Ficheaux. The presentation took place at British Headquarters in France in August. Private Proctor was the first man during the First World War to be so decorated on the battlefield. Born at 55 Church Street, Bootle in 1890 he was a pupil at St Mary's School. His VC is in the regimental collection in Liverpool.
- On September 2nd the Mayor unveiled a Roll of Honour to local men who had died so far in the First World War.
- On September 14th Dr William C. Minfie gave a 'cinematograph war lecture' entitled 'The British Fighting Forces in Camp and Field'.
- A clinic for expectant mothers was opened in November.
- A Supervisor of Supplies was appointed to visit schools to identify waste, particularly in lighting and heating.
- Electric lighting was installed in Bedford Road School and in all departments in Christ Church School except the Infants.
- The Education Committee asked magistrates, when granting licences for local cinemas, to require that children of school age should not be allowed in the cinema during school hours.
- The Orrell School Boy Scout troop published a magazine entitled 'Our Own'.
- All schools were closed at 3.30 p.m. so that cleaners could finish earlier and save on lighting.
- No. 4 Trinity Road became a Preparatory School associated with the Secondary School for Girls; there were 50 pupils on roll.
- The tower at Emmanuel Church in Stanley Road was dedicated.

1917

- Visit to the Borough by King George V and Queen Mary on May 14th. They viewed progress on the building of Gladstone Dock that had now restarted, using labour provided by German prisoners of war.
- In September St James' School Girls' Department was sub-divided into senior and junior

departments. Miss B. M. Brennan was appointed Headmistress of the Junior Girls.

- The Mayor, on behalf of the people of Bootle, presented a motor ambulance to the Bootle Hospital Committee on October 4th.
- Alderman Dr James Pearson was elected Mayor for the third time in November. He has the distinction of being the only person to have served three terms in office as Mayor of Bootle.
- The pupils of Balliol Council School raised £1,000 to purchase War Savings Certificates, a sum reached by only one other elementary school in the country.
- 'Economical Cooking' courses were provided for local housewives by the Technical School staff.
- Schoolchildren were given the task of sewing sacks for sandbags for military use.
- A proclamation by the King was read in all churches urging people to be wise and not wasteful in the use of bread owing to the war.

1918

- Bootle was constituted a Parliamentary Borough on February 6th by the Representation of the People Act, 1918.
- In April the Junior Technical College moved back to the Day Industrial School premises in Marsh Lane.
- The Mayor unveiled the second list of names on the Roll of Honour on the war memorial in Bootle Town Hall on Empire Day, May 24th.
- The Mayor presided at a Thanksgiving Meeting in the Town Hall on November 17th to celebrate the signing of the Armistice that marked the end of the First World War. Later in the month a Peace Day victory march took place, followed by a service in St Mary's Church.
- On December 14th the first election took place for the Member of Parliament for Bootle. Sir Thomas Royden of Frankby Hall, Cheshire, was elected. This was the first parliamentary election in which women were allowed to vote.
- Celebrations were held on December 30th to mark the 50th anniversary of the granting of the Charter of Incorporation of the Borough of Bootle.
- Opening of the Marsh Lane Social Institute for young men in December.
- No. 69 Balliol Road was purchased to house a Preparatory Department for the Boys' Secondary School
- The Mayor inaugurated the Juvenile Organisational Committee (JOC) local committee at a meeting in Marsh Lane Assembly Rooms. The organisation was set up to support young people's welfare.

1919

- From January male teachers began to be demobilised from the forces and they returned to their jobs. Married women teachers, who had 'held the fort' during hostilities, were made redundant.

- Sir Thomas Royden MP opened a new home for the Queen Victoria's Nursing Association at 57 Balliol Road on February 26th.
- Schools were closed for a day in February to enable local children to view a trophy gun captured by the King's (Liverpool) Regiment during the war.
- The Breeze Hill Auxiliary Military Hospital was closed in March.
- The first two women police officers were appointed to the Bootle Force in April.
- The Mayor held an Empire Day ball and whist drive in the Town Hall on May 14th. Profits from the venture were donated to St Dunstan's Hospital for blinded soldiers and sailors.
- Ten of the 21 houses in Laburnum Place were demolished in June to enable Bootle Tannery to be extended.
- Sir Thomas Royden MP unveiled a war memorial in St Leonard's Church on June 29th.
- A Thanksgiving service was held in Derby Park on July 6th to mark the signing of the peace treaty that ended the First World War.
- There was a public celebration of the declaration of peace in Europe from July 19th- 21st. A garden party was held in Derby Park and the 7th King's (Liverpool) Regiment led a victory march round the Borough. Bootle Municipal Military Band provided the music.
- In August the Corporation bought the land in Breeze Hill on which Hillside High School now stands.
- A police strike took place in Bootle in August. Premises were wrecked and looted; 63 policemen out of a force of 77 were sacked for failing to report for duty.
- August 28th-29th all schools closed for peace celebrations. On 28th the children of the Borough were entertained to a tea by the Mayor; the following day was declared a 'peace holiday'.
- On September 17th work started on the building of the first post-war housing in Bootle; the Mayor cut the first sod. The housing scheme, located in Orrell, was built under the 1919 Housing Act.
- The Bishop of Liverpool dedicated the memorial organ in St Leonard's C of E Church in Peel Road on October 4th.
- A memorial Roll of Honour was part of the war memorial unveiled in Bedford Council School on October 24th in memory of ex-pupils and staff.
- A. Bonar Law MP, Lord Privy Seal and Leader of the House of Commons, received the Freedom of the Borough of Bootle on October 31st. He was the first person to receive this honour.
- Christ Church C of E parish hall in Breeze Hill was reopened in November following its use by the military during the First World War.
- The first municipal election to be held since the end of the war took place on November 1st and was notable for two reasons. Firstly, Mrs Elizabeth Hannah Smith (Derby Ward) was the first woman to be elected to the Council under the Representation of the People's Act. Secondly, elected as a Labour Councillor for Knowsley Ward was Police Sergeant

Toolan, who had lost his job and pension after 32 years' service in the police due to his involvement in the police strike in August

- Miss R. Jackson, Matron of Bootle Hospital, inaugurated a 'Pound Day'. This made a contribution towards the cost of installing fire appliances and upgrading the hospital's electrical system.
- The National Relief Fund made a grant to Bootle Hospital of £1,450. This enabled the hospital authorities to wipe out the debt incurred in building the hospital.
- The Waterloo Division of the Red Cross presented Bootle Hospital with an ambulance.
- A fully staffed evening play centre was established in Bedford Road School with Miss E. Morgan as supervisor.
- Andrew & Irvine, saw millers, was founded at 5 Chesnut Grove.
- Taylor & Holmes, dynamo and motor manufacturers, opened premises at 2 Grimshaw Street.
- Bootle Corporation Gymnastic Team won the Bowring Shield awarded by the Liverpool and District Gymnasia League.

1920

- In February electric lighting was installed in Christ Church School's Infant department.
- Fire at Blackledge's bakery in Derby Road in February caused extensive damage.
- Memorial plaques in memory of scholars and staff who died in the First World War were unveiled in Linacre Council School on April 16th
- Admiral Sir John Reginald Tupper, Commander-in-Chief Western Approaches, unveiled the third list of 'The Fallen' in Bootle Town Hall on May 9th.
- The Royal Assent was given to the Bootle Corporation Act 1920 on August 4th,
- The 'Bootle Housing Bond Campaign' was inaugurated in October.
- New byelaws were inaugurated in October that prohibited the employment of any child less than 12 years of age, and limited work for the 12-14 year age group to an hour in the morning and an hour in the afternoon.
- A new Infant Welfare Clinic located in the Junior Technical School in Marsh Lane was opened in November.
- Sinn Fein placed a number of incendiary devices in local warehouses in November. The perpetrators were apprehended and received lengthy jail sentences.
- A club for men and boys was established at St John & St James Church. Later in the same year the 34th Liverpool Boys' Brigade Company was founded at the church.
- Bootle's attempt to extend its boundaries to include Litherland failed.
- Corkgrowers Trading Co. Ltd's Gerona Works was established in Vulcan Street.

1921

- The Census on June 20th showed 76,508 people living in Bootle.
- Edward, Prince of Wales, visited Bootle on July 5th as part of his Lancashire tour. The

Prince addressed a meeting of ex-servicemen in the Town Hall and inspected a guard of honour from 7th Battalion, King's (Liverpool) Regiment. Later he was shown round the works of Johnson's Cleaners & Dyers, and concluded with a visit to Hornby Dock. The local children were given a day off school so that they could line the streets and welcome him.

- In July the Broadway Cinema, previously The Picture House, was opened in Stanley Road, at the corner of Malvern Road. (The cinema was to be destroyed during the Blitz on May 8th 1941.)
- The name of the Prince's Theatre in Irlam Road was changed on September 19th to The Strand Cinema.
- Founding in November of the 170th Liverpool (St John's Bootle) Scout Group.
- Lady Bicket donated £550 to Bootle Hospital for the purchase of appliances in the electro-massage and orthopaedic department.
- Mrs Fred Burns donated £600 to Bootle hospital to pay for the installation of a lift.
- The Bootle JOC Football League was founded at Marsh Lane Social Institute for Young Men.
- The Penmaenmawr and Trinidad Lake Asphalt Co. Ltd was founded in Bootle.
- Arms and ammunition belonging to Sinn Fein were seized at a house in Bootle.

X00137910X album

18. Bootle War Memorial
Bootle War Memorial, unveiled 1922. It has an unusual design featuring an airman,
as well as a soldier and sailor, defending a mother and child.

1922

- A bronze plaque was unveiled in January by Viscountess Pirrie in the fitting shop of Harland and Wolff works, Regent Road. It was in memory of the 83 employees who died during the war.
- The Mayor opened the Municipal Maternity Home in Balliol Road on February 28th.
- The Mayor opened the Gainsborough Cinema in Knowsley Road in February. It had seating for 1,811 patrons. The first picture shown was 'The Love Flower'.
- On July 13th a further portion of the Borough Cemetery, set apart for interments, was consecrated. This was further extended in 1925.
- The town's War Memorial in Stanley Gardens was unveiled on October 15th by Major James Burnie MC. The memorial commemorated the 1,007 Bootle men who died during the First World War.
- Bootle Borough Hospital Service Guild was inaugurated.
- The British Oxygen Co. Ltd took over the site of Cook's Farm at the corner of Knowsley and Stanley Roads. The company remained here until 1939 when Bootle Corporation bought the site. (This is now the site of the Goddard Hall).
- Opening of a new canteen in Hawthorne Road by the British Women's Temperance Association.
- The Earl of Derby opened the Men's Memorial Club in Hornby Boulevard in memory of the employees of Bryant and May's Match Co. killed during the war.
- Messrs Gillett & Co Ltd. opened a boot-repairing factory at 226-8 Marsh Lane, next to the station.
- The Empire Picture Palace in Knowsley Road was converted into the Palais de Dance.

1923

- A holiday was given to all Bootle schoolchildren on April 26th to celebrate the marriage of the Duke and Duchess of York.
- On June 7th Royal Assent was given to the Bootle Corporation Act 1923 granting further powers to the Corporation as to rating of owners.
- In June, the first mention of building a school for St Monica's RC parish.
- The Apollo Cinema in Pembroke Road reverted to a public hall and was renamed County Hall on July 22nd.
- The Duke and Duchess of York visited Bootle Docks on July 25th; the Mayor and Mayoress were presented to them.
- Bootle dockers donated an ambulance to Bootle Hospital in August It was known affectionately as the 'Dockers' Ambulance'.
- Costigans' new central stores at 251-53 Stanley Road opened in September.
- A flagstaff was erected in Derby Park on September 25th in memory of Charles J. Byrne of Breeze Hill House. The inscription at the foot of the staff reads 'In memory of a happy life in Bootle'.

- The 7th Battalion, King's (Liverpool) Regiment handed in their colours to St Mary's Church for safe keeping on October 14th.
- A temporary church for the new parish of St Monica's was opened in November on the site now occupied by the presbytery. The parish priest was the Rev. B. Cain.
- The Bishop of Liverpool dedicated a memorial window in St Mary's Church in memory of the men of the parish who had lost their lives in the First World War.
- Founding of the 197th Liverpool (later 10th Bootle) Scout Group at St James' RC Church with Joseph Cope as Scoutmaster and William Leahy as Cubmaster. (The Boy Scout Association, in recognition of the boys who acted as messengers during the Second World War later awarded a Silver Cross to the troop. The group closed in 1964.)
- The Borough's Electricity Generating Station was sold to Liverpool Corporation, who henceforth supplied electricity to Bootle.
- A peal of bells was installed in St James' RC Church in memory of Canon Patrick L. Kelly who had served as parish priest for 35 years from 1887 to 1922.
- The Sun Hall Cinema in Stanley Road was renamed the Imperial Cinema.

1924

- Mann Street Bridewell closed in April.
- In August the JOC opened Markfield, a large house in Breeze Hill (where Hillside High School now stands) as a summer club.
- In November the managers of St Monica's RC Church accepted a tender for the building of a school in the parish.
- The Roman Catholic authorities acquired the premises known as Stanley Hall (on the site of what is now St Martin's House). The intention was to create a Central School for the more able Catholic boys aged 11-14 who lived in Bootle. It was later decided that the school would be an elementary school in the first instance

1925

- Alderman Sir Benjamin Johnson opened the new Liberal Club and Headquarters in Balliol Road in May.
- Exams were held on June 4th for entry into Balliol Road and St Joseph's Central Schools. Pupils aged ten but under twelve had to be recommended by their Headteachers in order to be able to sit the exam.
- The Archbishop of Liverpool laid the foundation stone of St Monica's RC School in Fernhill Road on September 6th.
- Following an increase of accidents to schoolchildren barriers were erected outside school gates.
- F. & W. Hughes opened a store at 95-7 Stanley Road in December, in premises previously occupied by the Grand Central Stores.
- The Bootle Estate Office that had been founded in 1884 became the firm of T. I. Phillips & Sons.

- Bootle Council acquired Orrell Public Pleasure Ground.
- Purchase of a motor trailer pump for the fire brigade. The pump was named 'Bellamy'.
- A Passionist Mission was held at St James' RC Church.
- Bootle electors decided not to support the Mersey Tunnel Bill.

1926

- The Archbishop of Liverpool opened St Joan of Arc RC School on April 29th. Headmistresses appointed were Miss Catherine Rafferty (Juniors) and Miss E. Wilcox (Infants).
- Albert Cleary, Chairman of the Bootle Trades Council and Labour Party, opened the Knowsley Road Labour Club on April 11th.
- In May work started on building a temporary wooden church for the newly-created parish of St Joan of Arc. The Archbishop of Liverpool consecrated the church on November 21st; Father H.V. O'Neill was appointed the first parish priest, a post he held until 1958. Father O'Neill had been a military chaplain, serving in France. During a visit to Rouen he had been inspired by the martyrdom of Joan of Arc. On demobilisation he persuaded the Archbishop of Liverpool to appoint him to a newly-created parish and to dedicate the church to St Joan of Arc.
- St Monica's RC School, Fernhill Road, opened on August 16th. It provided 300 places for infant and junior children. The school operated on the ground floor of the two-storey building, the upper floor being used for parish purposes. Miss B. Holohan was appointed Headmistress.
- On October 10th the Archbishop of Liverpool opened St Joseph's RC Central School (formerly Stanley Hall) in Balliol Road. Brother J. L. O'Leary was appointed Headmaster. This later became St Martin's RC Secondary School for Boys.
- The grounds in Breeze Hill that would eventually be the site of the Girls' Grammar School were laid out as playing fields for the use of the pupils of the secondary schools.
- New facilities at Orrell Council School enabled the teaching of laundry work in the winter and cookery in the summer.
- Following the publication of the Haddow Report, Bootle's Municipal Intermediate Day Schools became Secondary Schools.
- Miss Ethel M. Steuart was appointed Headmistress of Bootle Secondary School for Girls, Balliol Road. More than 50% of the pupils were fee-paying, many coming from the private preparatory school on the corner of Balliol and Pembroke Roads. The remaining pupils were from local schools, gaining entry through free scholarship places.
- The Bootle Disinfecting Fluid Co. Ltd was founded at 19-21 Litherland Road.
- The Mersey Cable Works Ltd opened premises in Linacre Lane.
- Members of the Old Girls' Association established a scholarship in memory of Miss Lydia Taylor, Headmistress of the Girls' Secondary School from 1910 to 1925.

1927

- In January Balliol Road School became a central school, admission being based on the passing of an examination. The pupils who were already in the school were allowed to remain, and work through the school. One of the consequences of becoming a central school was that the pupils were now drawn from many different parts of the Borough.
- The premises of the Bootle Warehouse Company in Pacific Road were gutted by fire on January 30th. Cotton to the value of £80,000 was destroyed. The Chief Fire Officer James Cecil Monk was killed during the incident: his funeral was held at St Mary's Church on February 4th.
- The Mayor brought into use a new refuse destructor that had been installed in Pine Grove.
- Councillor W.E. Hughes, Chairman of the Parks and Baths Committee, re-opened Marsh Lane Swimming Baths on May 30th following conversion from an open-air bath, and the installation of a circulating aerator and filtration plant.
- A total eclipse of the sun, visible in Bootle, occurred on Wednesday June 19th.
- A survey showed that 24 boys and 59 girls, all pupils at Balliol Central School, had to remain in school for their lunches because of the distance to their homes. It was anticipated that there would be a 50% increase in this number by the following year. As there were no facilities to serve hot lunches in school it was suggested that a hut be erected for this purpose.
- King George V and Queen Mary officiated at the opening of the final section of Gladstone Dock on July 19th. The King and Queen entered the dock standing on the bridge of the SS 'Galatea'.
- The Bishop of Liverpool dedicated a new choir vestry in St Mary's Church to mark the church's centenary.
- The Bishop of Liverpool laid the foundation stone of the parish hall of St John & St James' Church in Monfa Road on September 17th.
- Opening of the Bootle Masonic Hall in September on the corner of Balliol Road and Queens Road in premises previously used as St John's Vicarage.
- The Molyneux Rooms became the Employment Exchange in September.
- Read's Metal Box Co. established a factory in Orrell Lane.
- In September Linacre Park Presbyterian Church, Bailey Drive, was opened. A decision was taken by the Council to hire the church hall for use as a temporary Council School to provide places for 200 Infant and Junior children.

1928

- Roberts Temporary School opened on January 9th in the Presbyterian church hall. Mrs. Emily Pritchard was appointed Headmistress.
- In January discussions were held about the structure of exams for entry into post-elementary education – the Secondary and Central Schools. The exams were to be in two parts: the first to be carried out by Headteachers of the elementary schools and the second

by an independent outside body. The first exam for scholars aged between 10 years 8 months and 12 years 4 months was due on July 31st. To ensure a uniform standard for the first test a committee consisting of six Headteachers (2 Council, 2 C of E, 2 RC) plus the three Headteachers of the central schools was to set the first exam and fix the standard for marking. Children scoring 50% or above would be eligible to sit the second exam. However, in February it was decided that the National Union of Teachers (NUT) should set the first exam (English and arithmetic) which should not be as difficult as the second exam; the NUT would also draw up a marking schedule for Headteachers. The second exam would be conducted by the NUT at three centres: Linacre, Balliol and St Joseph's Schools. The candidates were to be selected in order of merit, firstly for places in the secondary schools and the remainder for the central schools.

- The King and Queen of Afghanistan visited Gladstone Dock in March and then attended the Grand National.

- Opening of the Jolly Farmer's Arms public house at 280 Marsh Lane in April. It was close to the site of the original inn that had stood at 211 Marsh Lane.

- The Earl of Derby officially opened the Penpoll Tin Smelting Works in Hawthorne Road on July 13th. It was the largest tin smelting works in Europe at that time.

- The Privy Council made an Order increasing the number of councillors on Bootle Council from 32 to 36, and the aldermen from 11 to 12.

- The Archbishop of Liverpool formally opened St Joan of Arc RC church hall and presbytery on November 23rd. Father O'Neill, the parish priest, was the grandson of the owner of the Argyle Theatre in Birkenhead. He used his theatrical background and contacts to organise spectacular pageants involving street processions. The pageants became famous and people travelled great distances to watch them. They continued until the start of the Second World War.

- Founding of the 179th Liverpool (later 7th Bootle) Scout Group at Ash Street Baptist Church. The first Group Scoutmaster was Mr Wright who ran a travel company in Stanley Road. (The troop was later awarded a Silver Cross by the Boy Scout Association for service by the boys who acted as messengers during the Second World War.)

- An evening institute was established in Bedford Road School with Mr F. C. Boardman as Headmaster. This enabled children over the age of fourteen to continue their education after gaining employment.

- Hornby Lighthouse known as the 'Bootle Bull', a foghorn on the north wall of Hornby Dock, was demolished. A lighthouse built on the north wall of Gladstone Dock replaced it.

- The Education Committee discussed corporal punishment and it was confirmed that Headteachers could administer six strokes of the cane to individual pupils and all Assistants, with the Headteacher's permission, could administer four.

- A covered porch was erected at the front of Bootle Hospital, the cost being met by the Bootle Hospital Service Guild.

19. St. James's School: senior boys 1929.

B1332

1929

- In March overcrowding in Orrell Council School was so great that the corridors had to be used as classrooms.

- The Archbishop of Liverpool opened Iona House, the Knights of St Columba Club, in Balliol Road on November 18th.

- On Christmas Day at Balliol Road Baths 1,025 hot pots were distributed to the poor.

- The Council purchased 18.5 acres of land that would eventually become Stuart Road Playing Fields.

- Hebron Hall in Akenside Street was hired at a cost of £50 per annum on nine half days per week for use by Gray Street Council School for physical education and drill lessons.

- Founding of the Rotary Club of Bootle and Litherland in the Wyndham Hotel, Oriel Road. The first president was Rev. Canon Edward Mayson, Vicar of Christ Church.

- The Council purchased a new Dennis motor turbine fire engine and named it 'Webster' in honour of the Chairman of the Fire Brigade Committee.

- G. Lawrenson and Sons based in Hawthorne Road founded the Merseyside Touring Co Ltd. The firm's fleet of charabancs took local people on tours to many parts of the country.

- Opening of Thomas Scott's new Empire Bread Bakery at 130-156 Knowsley Road.

1930

- The Walnut Tree Public House in Orrell Road was opened on February 12th.
- The Borough Hospital was renamed Bootle General Hospital on February 23rd.
- Woolworth's Store at 273-277 Stanley Road was opened on March 8th.
- In March milk was provided for the schoolchildren at a cost of a halfpenny a day.
- The Mayor laid the foundation stone of the Bootle Secondary School for Girls in Breeze Hill on May 21st. It was built at a cost of £50,000 on land once occupied by Markfield, a large mansion.
- Bedford Road School Senior Boys' and Girls' departments closed and the pupils transferred to Balliol Road Council School in September. Three Headteachers were appointed for the new primary school: Mr Samuel Donaldson (Boys), Miss E. E. Green (Girls) and Miss Roberta Tate (Infants).
- As part of September's reorganisation the senior boys from Christ Church and St John's Schools transferred to St Mary's School. The senior girls from St Mary's and St John's transferred to Christ Church School. St John's became a primary school (infants and juniors).
- In November it was decided to lease land in the Fernhill Road area for private housing development
- In December meals were delivered for the first time from the central kitchen to some of the outlying schools: Hawthorne Road, St Monica's, St John's, St Mary's and St Winefride's. The fire brigade provided the transport.
- The stepped galleries with bench seats, a feature of many schools' classrooms dating from the Victorian era, were removed. New dual desks replaced the old furniture.
- Schools that had spare capacity were allowed to create a nursery class for children under five years of age.
- Sandon, a house in Formby, was bought and furnished as a holiday home for Bootle children. (The following year Bootle Council inaugurated an annual camp for poor children. The camp catered for 800 children (up to 50 per week) over a 10-14 week period during the summer.)
- The Bootle Weight Training Club was formed.

1931

- On February 18th a decision was taken to employ a local Inspector of Schools: Mr W.H. Otter was appointed.
- The Earl of Derby laid the foundation stone of a new Outpatients' Department at Bootle Hospital on February 20th.
- The census taken on April 26th showed 76,800 people living in Bootle.
- The Chairman of the Education Committee, Alderman James R. Barbour, officially opened Roberts Council School on June 26th. The school was named to mark the service and perpetuate the memory of Alderman Dr R.E. Roberts. The Headteachers were appointed were Mr E. J. Pengelly (Senior Boys), Miss Mabelle Bond (Senior Girls) and Mrs Eleanor Kay (Juniors and Infants).

- Roberts Temporary School operating in the Presbyterian Institute closed on July 10th.
- On November 4th the Prince of Wales visited Hornby Dock where local dignitaries were presented to him.
- In November the Housecraft Centre in Bedford Road School was updated when a gas iron heater, gas boiler and slop sink were installed.
- The number of pupils on the roll of St Monica's School exceeded the 500 ceiling placed there by the Education Committee. In response the Headmistress asserted that the weekly attendance never exceeded 486!
- St James' Select School became a Junior Mixed school.
- North-Western Developments Ltd., started building the Fernhill Road / Aintree Road estate.
- Founding of the 12th Bootle Scout Group in Roberts Council School with Mr Ainsworth as GSM. The group later built their own headquarters in Captain's Lane. (The Boy Scout Association subsequently awarded the troop a Silver Cross in recognition of the bravery shown by the boys who acted as messengers during the Second World War.)
- The Metropole Theatre in Stanley Road was converted to 'cine-variety'.
- The Palais de Dance in Knowsley Road was converted to the Bootle Trades and Labour Club.

20. New Outpatients' Department
New Outpatients' Department opened in the Borough Hospital, 1932. The official party, led by Bootle's MP, Colonel Chichester de Windt Crookshank, inspect the operating theatre.

1932

- On March 4th Chichester de Windt Crookshank MP opened the new Outpatients' Department at Bootle Hospital, built at a cost of £25,000.
- The Earl of Derby opened the newly built Secondary School for Girls in Breeze Hill on April 8th. With the departure of the Secondary Girls' Department to the Breeze Hill site the Junior Technical School in Marsh Lane was relocated to the main Technical School site.
- Sir George Newman, Chief Medical Officer to the Board of Education, opened a new Health Centre in Knowsley Road on June 7th.
- St Joseph's RC Central Elementary School for Boys in Stanley Road, run by the Xavier Brothers, closed in August The school re-opened on September 8th as St Martin's RC College, a secondary school for boys under the direction of the Salesian Brothers. The school catered for boys from Bootle's Catholic elementary schools who passed the selection examination. Successful girls went either to Seafield in Crosby or Notre Dame in Liverpool.
- St Robert Bellarmine's RC Church had its beginnings in a stable loft at the rear of 24 Alexandra Drive. The first parish priest was Rev. Fr. Robert Coupe and the first Mass was celebrated on August 29th. In September the church moved to Bibby's Sports Pavilion in Orrell Lane.
- From September the practice at the Boys' Secondary School of having lessons on Saturday mornings and a half-day holiday on a Wednesday was discontinued; it was replaced by a Monday to Friday timetable.
- During the year the Footwear Fund issued 1,076 pairs of free clogs to needy children.
- Because of pressure of space Roberts Council School had once more to hire two classrooms in the Bailey Drive Presbyterian Institute.
- The Orrell and District Veterans' Association (ODVA) was founded. Prior to opening their own headquarters in Fernhill Road they met in Roberts Council School.
- Station Officer Mark Edey of the Borough Fire Brigade was killed while attending a shop fire in Marsh Lane.
- Immunisation against diphtheria was introduced for all Bootle schoolchildren.

1933

- The Mayor opened Bootle Stadium in Aintree Road on June 3rd. The building of the stadium provided much needed work for local unemployed men.
- The Archbishop of Liverpool laid the foundation stone of St Robert Bellarmine's RC Church on September 17th.
- Bootle Village Pipe Band was established.
- Bootle Technical School was re-designated Bootle Technical College.
- Formation of the Bootle Jazz Band.
- Bootle Hospital's X-ray Department was modernised and transferred to a spacious new suite of rooms in the old Outpatients' Department.

21. Mayor James Scott at the opening of Bootle Stadium, 1933.

B1486

1934

- The Mayor re-opened the Central Library, Museum and Art Gallery to the public in January after the buildings had been enlarged and extensively reorganised.
- The Mayor opened Bootle Municipal Golf Course on May 19th.
- On July 18th the Mayor of Bootle and other local dignitaries were presented to King George V and Queen Mary on the occasion of the royal visit to Liverpool to open the Mersey Tunnel.
- In August Balliol Road School Junior and Infant department was closed and the children were transferred to Bedford Road School.
- In September Hawthorne Road School's older pupils transferred to Balliol Road School. The Headteachers appointed to the new primary school were Mr E. Preston (Boys), Miss Elizabeth Logan (Girls) and Miss Annie Filshie (Infants).
- The Aintree Hotel in Aintree Road was opened on September 21st.
- Two houses in Merton Road were linked to form the Merton Hotel. It was formally opened on December 13th.
- The Bootle Teachers' Association requested that the rule requiring teachers employed by Bootle Council to live within the Borough be lifted. It was declined.
- The Archbishop of Liverpool consecrated St Robert Bellarmine's RC Church.

22. The Cabbage Inn
The Cabbage Inn, Netherton, was rebuilt in 1934.

B631

- Pastor Edward Jeffries held a faith-healing crusade in a large tent (capable of holding 3,000 people) on what was then a brickfield adjacent to Breeze Hill. The following January the Bethel Full Gospel Church, known to some as Bootle's Wooden Cathedral, was built nearby in Southport Road.
- The Cabbage Inn, Netherton, was reopened after major refurbishment. An inn bearing this unusual name had stood on this site for 260 years. Local tradition has it that the original innkeeper was also a tailor. The O.E.D. has an entry indicating that to cabbage means to pilfer, originally said of a tailor appropriating part of the cloth given to him to make up into garments - is this we wonder the origin of the inn's name?
- The Metropole in Stanley Road reverted to being a theatre.

1935

- In January there was a request that the stones once used to sharpen the pupils' slate pencils be removed from the grounds of Balliol Road School.
- St Robert Bellarmine's RC School was opened on January 5th and Mr D. Kirby was appointed Headmaster.
- Mr Warwick M. Bolam was appointed Bootle's first Director of Education in January on a salary of £700 per annum, later rising to £900.

- The Mayor opened Stuart Road Playing Fields on February 22nd.
- A House of Lords Committee of Enquiry that sat from March 19th to 28th rejected Bootle Corporation's attempt (through a Parliamentary Bill) to extend its boundaries to incorporate Great Crosby, Seaforth, Litherland, Waterloo and the townships of Ford, Netherton and Sefton.
- St Joan of Arc RC Junior and Infant School was opened in April. Headmistresses appointed: Miss Catherine Rafferty, Junior Mixed, and Miss E. Wilcox (Sister Mary), Infants.
- A special holiday was granted to all Bootle schoolchildren on May 6th to mark the Silver Jubilee of King George V and Queen Mary. This was followed by a united thanksgiving service in the Town Hall on May 12th.
- On June 2nd a wooden cross from the grave on an Unknown Soldier in Flanders was mounted next to the war memorial in Christ Church at a special ceremony.
- In November for the first time a grant was made from the rates towards the provision of school meals.
- Bootle became a Registration District and an office was opened at 2 Trinity Road. Mr W.G.H. Forest was appointed as the first Superintendent Registrar, authorised to conduct civil marriages. Previously only births and deaths could be registered in the Borough, in an office at 77 Merton Road.
- The first traffic roundabout in Bootle was built at the junction of Knowsley Road, Linacre Lane and Stanley Road.

1936

- The new building for St James' RC Senior School was officially opened on January 7th. The younger pupils now used the buildings previously used by the senior children.
- The Mayor made a public proclamation of the accession of King Edward VIII on January 23rd. This was followed by a memorial service for King George V held in St Mary's Church on January 28th.
- The Mayor opened Miller's Bridge Children's Playground on March 17th. The playground, built on land previously occupied by a timber yard, included a paddling pool and swings.
- On April 20th the Mayor opened a Junior Instruction Centre for boys in Marsh Lane. The building had previously been used by the Junior Technical College. Mr W. H. Bolton was appointed Superintendent.
- Alderman Joseph S. Kelly, Chairman of the Parks and Baths Committee, opened the children's playground in the North Recreation Ground on June 16th.
- On August 29th the Mayor opened a new sports' pavilion at Orrell Pleasure Ground.
- On December 15th the Mayor made a local proclamation from the steps of the Town Hall to announce the accession of King George VI.
- Miss O. M. Evans was appointed the first Almoner at Bootle Hospital.
- Founding of the 330th Liverpool (later 14th Bootle) Boy Scout troop at Gray Street Council School. The first Scoutmaster was Mr A.T. Bruns.

- Founding of the 365th Liverpool (later 15th Bootle) Sea Scout troop with headquarters at 69 Balliol Road. The first Scoutmaster was Rev. A. Sloerfin. This was sponsored by Bootle Boys' Secondary School.
- Founding of the 16th Bootle Boy Scout Group at Queens Road Undenominational Church, with Mr Joe Pugh as Scoutmaster. The group later moved to St Paul's and Trinity Presbyterian Church in Hawthorne Road, where Mr Eric Clayton was Scoutmaster and his wife Phyllis was Cubmaster. When the church closed in 1980 the group moved to Gloucester Road Youth Centre.
- The Primitive Methodist Church in Queens Road was closed and became an Undenominational Mission.
- The Archbishop of Liverpool opened St Monica's RC Church in Fernhill Road. The church, designed by F. X. Verlarde was built at a cost of £18,000.

1937

- A special holiday was granted to all Bootle pupils from May 12th-18th to mark the Coronation of King George VI and Queen Elizabeth. Sixpence per head was allocated to pay for parties on May 11th. Commemorative mugs were presented to all elementary school children and brooches and tiepins to the secondary pupils. A number of local bands played in the parks including 7th Battalion King's (Liverpool) Regiment, Tom Hughes' Bedford Orchestra, John L. Pennington's Orchestra, the Liverpool Subscription Military Band, the Dingle Silver Prize Band and the 87th Liverpool Scout Group Silver Band.
- The Mayor opened a Children's Playground in South Recreation Ground on June 9th.
- The Council's Municipal Midwifery Service was established on July 1st
- King George VI and Queen Elizabeth visited Bootle on July 11th.
- Alderman Simon Mahon officially opened the newly constructed Coffee House Bridge on December 16th.
- The foundation stone of St Richard of Chichester's RC Church, Miranda Road, was laid.
- Following the death of Sir Benjamin Sands Johnson, who had served as Chairman of the Hospital Committee from 1914-16, a bed in the hospital was endowed in his memory. The cost was met by donations from the employees of Johnson Bros. Dyers Ltd and members of the Hospital Committee.

1938

- The Bootle section of the Air Raid Precautions (ARP) Wardens was formed in January. The Clerk to the Justices, Mr Frank Preston, was appointed Chief Warden.
- In March two classes of senior pupils from St Monica's RC School were accommodated in the old parish church building, and a further class in St James' Select School.
- St Monica's Boys' School in Aintree Road was officially opened on April 25th. Mr W. Heyes, previously Headmaster of St James' Select School, was appointed Headmaster of the new school.
- Councillor S. Williams, Deputy Chairman of the Parks and Baths' Committee, opened a

23. Telephone Exchange
In 1934 Mayor Maurice Webster made an official visit to the town's telephone exchange.

Children's Playground in Recreation Street on May 14th.
- The Mayor opened Derby Road Bowling Green on May 14th.
- King George VI and Queen Elizabeth visited Bootle on May 19th and a large party of local dignitaries were presented to them in front of the Town Hall. Among those presented were Gladys Marshall and Kenneth Rigby, representing the children of Bootle. Kenneth was the captain of the Bootle Schoolboys Football Team.
- Founding of the Bootle Club of Soroptimist International in July.
- The Archbishop of Liverpool consecrated St Richard of Chichester's RC Church in Miranda Road on July 31st as a Chapel of Ease to St Alexander's Church.
- The Senior Girls' Department at Christ Church School and the Senior Boys' Department at St Mary's School were closed; the pupils transferred to Balliol Road Council School in September.
- The foundations of a Branch Library in Linacre Lane, Orrell, were laid. (With the outbreak of war, work on the building was suspended. The steel skeleton of the uncompleted building stood on the site until 1955.)
- A decision was taken to build a senior department for St Joan of Arc School. (Plans were put in hand but work did not begin because of the outbreak of war. The school was built after the war and the raconteur Peter Maloney served on the staff. Around the same time

24. King George VI

King George VI (seen facing left, in front of the phone box) reviewing the 7th Battalion, King's (Liverpool) Regiment, outside the Town Hall during the 1938 royal visit. The station building in the background, though in Oriel Road, is the entrance to Balliol Road Station, since demolished. (Photo courtesy Cull Micro Imaging)

the comedian Tom O'Connor taught in the Junior Department.)

- Founding of the Northfield Road Gospel Hall (corner of Northfield Road and Linacre Lane) in a building previously known as Henderson Hall.

1939

- On January 8th Miss E. Penhall, President of the Women's Section of the Bootle Branch of the British Legion unveiled a memorial cross in St Mary's Church to an Unknown Soldier.
- The National Unemployed Workers' Movement (NUWM) held a lie-down demonstration in Rimrose Road on January 24th. On the same day the Mayor inaugurated a National Service scheme for the Borough.
- Alderman Simon Mahon, Chairman of the Housing and Town Planning Committee, laid the first brick of a housing scheme in Aintree Road on February 8th. The scheme comprised 54 houses.

- Because of its proximity to the docks Bootle Hospital was moved to the Linacre Lane Fever Hospital site in March where it remained for the duration of the war.
- The first ARP exercises took place in the Borough on March 31st
- Alderman James Maguire officially opened Southport Road, between Brewster Street and Oxford Road, on April 25th.
- Balliol Road Baths were officially reopened after renovation on May 2nd.
- Following the declaration of war on September 3rd, 6,189 children were evacuated from Bootle. The same month identity cards were issued to everyone following national registration, and regulations were introduced requiring all windows to be blacked out after dark.
- From September Linacre Council School became a primary school catering for children up to the age of eleven. Headteachers were Mr John Dickinson (Boys), Miss Annie Griffiths (Girls) and Miss Mary McPhearson (Infants). The older pupils transferred to Gray Street or Roberts Council Schools' senior departments.
- On September 13th the Earl of Derby visited the Borough to inspect the progress made in dealing with the National Emergency.
- On November 1st Municipal Elections were suspended for the duration of the war.
- On November 17th the air raid warning was sounded for the first time.
- In December it was decided to provide air-raid shelters for all schools and an Evacuation Welfare Committee was established in Southport.
- First-aid posts were established at Linacre and Hawthorne Road Council Schools, and at Quarry Bank (a house in Balliol Road).
- Marsh Lane Baths was set aside for use as an emergency mortuary.
- Auxiliary Fire Stations were established at Orrell Lodge, Gray Street School, West Langton Dock, Alexandra Dock, Knowsley Road ARP Depot, Bootle Cricket Club and Bootle Stadium.
- A trailing cable from a barrage balloon became entangled in the spire of St Mary's Church, causing the top of the spire to become detached and fall through the roof of the church.
- A new road known as Caterpillar Close was created in the garden of St Andrew's Vicarage. It consisted of seven or eight air-raid shelters belonging to the houses in St Andrew's Road.
- Bootle's boundaries were extended to include parts of Ford, Sefton and Netherton.
- The pupils from Bootle Secondary School for Boys were evacuated to Southport.

1940

- After a period of closure, during which most children were evacuated, schools reopened in January and the end of the school day was extended from 3.15 p.m. to 4 p.m.
- The Earl of Derby opened the Flotilla Club in Gladstone Dock on January 11th.
- A surprise visit by King George VI and Queen Elizabeth to Bootle on May 1st.
- The town's first fire float was launched on July 3rd and was named the 'James Spence' after the Mayor.

- On July 23rd the Bishop of Liverpool and the Rev. S. F. Sullivan consecrated land as Service Graves in the Borough Cemetery.
- The Mayor opened an exhibition of war photographs in St John's Church Hall on July 26th.
- The first bombs fell on Bootle during the nights of August 29th-30th.
- The Technical College suffered war damage in October and the pupils were transferred to the Junior Instruction Centre in Irlam Road.
- A temporary Branch Library was established in Stanley Road in October.
- Alderman Joseph Sylvester Kelly, popularly known as the 'Tin Hat Mayor', was elected Mayor in November.
- King George VI and Queen Elizabeth visited Bootle on November 7th. They viewed the bomb damage and met local dignitaries and rescue workers,
- A parachute mine destroyed the Protestant Free Church, Trinity Road, on November 28th.
- Five Bootle firemen were killed at Alexandra Dock while fire fighting on December 22nd.
- Public air-raid shelters were erected in many streets and nos. 2 and 4 Trinity Road were used as emergency shelters for people at Balliol Road baths.
- During the war a dormitory was set up at Bootle Town Hall, the nerve centre of the Civil Defence authorities.
- Founding of the 17th Bootle Scout Group at Bethel Baptist church with Mr Harold Rhodes as Group Scoutmaster.
- Responsible local householders were given keys to the communal air-raid shelters. Their role was to open the shelters when the air-raid warning sounded and close them after the 'All Clear'.
- Bootle took up the option to use Marton Camp at Whitegate near Northwich, Cheshire, as an evacuation centre for Bootle schoolchildren. Eleven teachers and 290 boys were evacuated to Marton during the war.

1941

- The first presentation of Honours in the town took place on January 20th when Warden Archibald Lennie was awarded the George Medal.
- The 29th January saw the opening of National Savings 'War Weapons Week'. Lord Crawford and Lord Derby visited the Borough to support the scheme.
- The Home Secretary, Robert Morrison, visited the Borough on February 14th to inspect war damage.
- All Bootle schools closed during the May Blitz because of the heavy bombing.
- During the May Blitz (May 2nd-9th) there was concentrated bombing of the town: 74% of Bootle's houses were destroyed or damaged; 1,000 people were killed or injured; 20,000 people were made homeless.
- During the May Blitz many public buildings and places of worship were damaged as a result of bombing and subsequent fires. St Mary's C of E Church in Irlam Road was gutted by fire, and services were held in the school buildings. St Leonard's C of E Church and church hall in Peel Road were destroyed, and services were held in the Vicarage until a temporary building was erected; St Alexander's RC Church in St John's Road was wrecked. St Joan of Arc Primary School and the Men's Club were bombed; nearby houses were destroyed and many people killed. St Andrew's C of E church hall and the Branch Library in Marsh Lane both suffered bomb damage.
- Following the May Blitz further evacuation of children took place to Cheshire, Radnorshire, Herefordshire, Shropshire and Southport. In all 1,553 pupils were involved.
- Pupils from some of the Roman Catholic schools were evacuated to Haydock and Wigan.
- The pupils and staff of St Martin's RC College were evacuated to Coalbrookdale in Shropshire. Pupils of St Winefride's RC School used St Martin's College buildings.
- On May 16th there was a communal burial of air raid victims in Bootle Cemetery.
- Local fire brigades were nationalised and became part of the National Fire Service on August 18th.
- The Minister of Food Lord Woolton, visited Bootle on August 24th to inspect the emergency feeding arrangements in the Borough. Emergency feeding stations had been set up in Orrell, Balliol Road, Hawthorne Road and Roberts Schools in sheds in the schoolyards.
- The Mayor officially opened the British Restaurants on October 6th. These community dining rooms were set up in the Cocoa Rooms, Victoria House in Strand Road and at 223 and 376-380 Stanley Road.
- King George VI paid a surprise visit to the Borough on October 8th to make a lightning tour of Naval establishments.
- Enemy bombing destroyed Thomas Scott's Bakery in Knowsley Road.
- Marsh Lane Baths, which had been converted into a temporary mortuary, was bombed.
- Bootle's only theatre, the Metropole, was destroyed by enemy action.
- County Hall in Pembroke Road was partly destroyed by enemy action. (It was never rebuilt and was demolished in 1950.)
- The last air raid on Bootle occurred on October 20th.
- First aid depots were established at Quarry Bank, 47 Balliol Road and at St James' Select School.
- St Paul's Presbyterian Church in Peel Road was badly damaged. The congregation joined the congregation of Trinity Presbyterian Church for worship. (In time Trinity Church became known as St Paul's and Trinity.)
- Mr Alec Fletcher, Headmaster of Roberts Senior Boys' Department, was seconded to the Education Office to supervise the registration and organisation of young people between the ages of 16 and 18. Subsequently the Sea Cadets, Army Cadets and the Girls' Training Corps were established. The youth organisations at Ash Street Baptist, St Mary's and St Leonard's churches began meeting again.
- Arrangements were made for children belonging to uniformed organisations to receive extra clothing coupons to purchase their uniforms.
- The Girls' Department of Linacre School was used for a time as a mortuary; Bedford Road School was used to store household furniture belonging to Blitz victims.

MWD-31

25. The May Blitz 1941
The May Blitz 1941: looking down Marsh Lane from Rimrose Road. (Photo courtesy National Museums Liverpool)

- A temporary Branch Library for Orrell was opened in a shop in Linacre Lane.
- There were now Auxiliary Fire Stations at Orrell Lodge, Gray Street School, Downing's Garage, Bootle Stadium, Knowsley Road ARP depot, Bootle Cricket Club pavilion, North and South Gladstone Docks, Houlder Bros. berth, the west side of Langton Dock and the south side of Alexandra No. 2 Dock.
- George Medals were awarded to Chief Inspector Alexander Ross of the Bootle Police Force and Senior Warden James C. Pickering, an official in the Bootle Rates Department. They entered property in Morningside Road that was in danger of collapse and rescued the occupants.
- St Matthew's church hall, which had escaped damage during the Blitz, was used as an emergency refuge for people whose homes had been destroyed or badly damaged.

26. Mobile Canteen
A mobile canteen, presented to Bootle in 1942 by the brewers Walker of Warrington and Cain of Liverpool. The Mayor is Joseph Riley.

1942

- Hergest Croft, a large house in Kington, Herefordshire, was prepared to receive the pupils and staff of the Bootle Secondary School for Girls. The centre was officially opened in May.
- On July 1st Captain Johnny Walker presented the Corporation with HMS Stork's battle ensign
- In September 1939 there had been 17,119 dwelling houses in Bootle. A survey showed that, during the Blitz, 2,017 houses were totally destroyed, 6,000 were seriously damaged and 8,000 superficially damaged.

- A mobile canteen was presented to the town's Women's Voluntary Service on October 15th. It was the gift of two local brewing companies, Walker's of Warrington and Cain's of Liverpool.
- On October 17th an exchange of plaques between HMS Erne and Bootle Council took place, in connection with Warships Week.
- Eleanor Roosevelt the wife of the American President visited the Borough on November 8th.
- A Council of Youth was inaugurated in November.
- King George VI and Queen Elizabeth visited Bootle on November 18th. They inspected the first 'super rest-centre' to be constructed in the country, located in Kirby Road, Orrell.
- The pupils and staff of St Martin's RC College, evacuated to Coalbrookdale in 1941, moved to Blackpool. There they joined the staff and pupils of St Francis Xavier School, Manchester.
- Work began in Dunnings Bridge Road on the building of new premises for Thomas Scott's bakery.
- A public shelter in Breeze Hill was made available to pupils attending the Girls' Secondary School.
- Wesley Hall in Sheridan Place was closed.
- St Leonard's parish's congregation was provided with a temporary church building.

1943

- The ensigns of HMS Hesperus and HMS Erne were presented to the Council on March 1st
- On May 15th Lady Baden Powell, the Chief Guide, visited Bootle.
- The crew of HMS Bootle donated £40 for the benefit of the children of Hawthorne Road Council School.
- A prefabricated hut was built behind St Monica's School for use as a nursery and air raid shelter.
- The nursing staff that had used part of Roberts Council School senior department for sleeping accommodation moved to new accommodation on the Linacre Hospital site.

1944

- Captain Johnny Walker, Commander of the 36th Escort Group based in Bootle, presented the Corporation with the battle flags and 'General Chase' flags of HMS Starling and HMS Kite on January 5th.
- In July Captain Walker died of a stroke. His funeral was held in Liverpool Anglican Cathedral and he was buried at sea in sight of Bootle Docks.
- The battle flag flown by the minesweeper HMS Bootle when she went into action off the coast of Normandy on D-Day was presented to the Mayor on August 5th.
- On December 29th the air raid warning siren sounded in Bootle for the 502nd and final time.
- In December Robert Mason a pupil at St Monica's Senior Boys School won the Northern Counties Junior Amateur Boxing Championship in Birkenhead.
- Marton Camp at Whitegate near Northwich was closed.
- The Bootle Evening Townswomen's Guild was founded.
- Marsh Lane Baths were reopened.

27. Captain Johnny Walker

War hero Captain Johnny Walker presents the 'General Chase' signal to
Mayor George Rogers at the Town Hall, 1944.

B826

1945

- The Mayor opened the new Branch Library in Peel Road on February 28th.
- Street parties were held in May to celebrate victory in Europe.
- Following a decision to rename the Bootle May Day celebrations 'Bootle Carnival', Marjorie Jay was installed as the Victory Queen at the carnival in May.
- On October 5th the Residential Nursery, Grangewood in Formby, was formally taken over by Bootle Council.
- The Mayor opened the Women's Voluntary Service (WVS) Clothing Exchange on November 11th.
- With the return of evacuees the number of pupils on roll at Roberts Primary School swelled to 400. A temporary annexe was once again opened in nearby St Stephen's Church to cater for the extra numbers.
- Founding of the 11th Bootle Boy Scout Group at St Paul's Presbyterian Church in Peel Road. The group met in Salisbury Road School.
- Founding of the 20th Bootle Boy Scout group in the Olivet Mission Hall, Marsh Lane, with Mr James Scott as Scoutmaster.

1946

- In June Eden Vale, a large house on the corner of Breeze Hill and Hawthorne Road was purchased and adapted to accommodate four classes from Christ Church C of E Junior School.
- On September 6th the Mayor opened Connolly House in Balliol Road as a home for 17 blind people. It was named after Councillor T. Connolly, a former chairman of the Blind Welfare Committee, to commemorate his work for visually-impaired people.
- The Elizabeth Walker Memorial Eventide Home was opened in Orrell Road on September 11th.
- The Merton Hotel reopened in November. During the war the American Army had requisitioned it.
- Wilfred Pickles and his radio show 'Have a Go' was broadcast from Roberts Council School on December 30th.
- The children of Christ Church School commenced using Christ Church Mission Hall in Waterworks Street as a dinner centre.
- In line with the requirements of the 1944 Education Act the Secondary School for Boys based in the Technical School, Balliol Road, became Bootle Grammar School for Boys, and the Secondary School for Girls, Breeze Hill, became Bootle Grammar School for Girls.
- Distinctive uniforms were introduced into the two grammar schools, including school badges bearing the Borough's coat of arms. Means-tested grants were made available for pupils attending these schools to aid the purchase of school uniforms.
- A memorial scholarship in memory of the late Captain Johnny Walker was instituted. It was designed to enable boys to take up places on HMS Conway, the Royal Navy's cadet training ship.
- Due to a shortage of qualified teachers Bootle offered temporary employment to people who had been accepted for teacher training as part of the Government's Emergency Training Scheme. The cost of the staff was met by central government.
- Founding of the 9th Bootle Scout Group at St Andrew's Church with Tom Vivienne as Scoutmaster.
- Three cinemas remained in Bootle, two others having been destroyed by enemy action. The surviving cinemas were the Gainsborough in Knowsley Road, the Imperial in Stanley Road and the Palace in Marsh Lane.
- In its centenary year Bootle Hospital became part of the National Health Service, under the control of the North Liverpool Hospital Management Committee of the Liverpool Regional Hospital Board.
- The YMCA opened a Boys' Club in the basement hall of the Victoria British Restaurant in Strand Road.

1947

- The Linacre Hospital site became available for educational purposes in early March. In April the senior boys and girls of St Monica's and St Robert Bellarmine's schools plus the Domestic Science and Handicraft centres at Orrell School were moved to the site.
- The school-leaving age was raised to 15 in April. A variety of steps were taken to provide

28. Peel Road Library
In 1945 Mayor William Keenan opened a branch library in Peel Road.

B320

teaching space for the extra pupils. For example the 14-year-old pupils from St James' Secondary Modern School were accommodated in basement rooms in St Martin's RC College in Stanley Road.

- In June two classes from Bedford Road Infants moved into Quarry Bank, a large house in Balliol Road.
- In June numbers 188 and 190 Rimrose Road were purchased to enable St Joan of Arc RC School to be extended.
- In August the bomb-damaged Metropole Theatre in Stanley Road was demolished.
- From August free milk was provided in schools for all primary and secondary children. The cost of the milk was met by central government.
- Founding of the 22nd Bootle (Christ Church) Boy Scout Group with Len Lloyd as GSM. The group met in Bedford Road Council School until 1967 when they moved to Christ Church parish hall.
- Temporary classrooms were erected on the site of 7 St John's Road to accommodate infants from St Winefride's RC School.
- Two classes of junior boys from to Orrell School, who had been using the Kirby Road Rest Centre, returned to the main school building.

- The air-raid shelters in the grounds of St Monica's and Bedford Road Schools were removed.
- Two huts were erected in St John's Road for pupils from St Alexander's parish. They formed part of St Winefride's RC Infant School.
- Senior pupils from Gray Street School were accommodated on the Linacre Hospital site.
- The Earl of Derby re-opened Bootle Borough Hospital on its Derby Road site.
- The WVS inaugurated a Meals-on-Wheels Service in Bootle.
- Bootle Chamber of Commerce was established.

1948

- On March 19th Bootle elected its first Children's Mayor, Rita Murphy, a pupil at St James' RC School.
- The National Fire Service ended in April and Bootle took over its fire brigade once more. Mr A. J. Greenslade was appointed Chief Fire Officer.
- The 40th Royal Tank Regiment, better known as 'Monty's Foxhounds' was granted the Freedom of the Borough of Bootle on May 22nd. This gave it the right to enter and march through the town on all ceremonial occasions with drums beating, colours flying and bayonets fixed.
- The remains of St Mary's C of E Church in Irlam Road were demolished in June.
- The first radar system in the world to guide ships into a port was installed in Gladstone Dock in July.
- The foundation stone of the Bootle Protestant Free Church in Trinity Road was laid on September 18th. The original church had been destroyed in the May 1941 Blitz.
- Founding of the 18th Bootle Air Scouts, sponsored by the Bootle Grammar School for Boys. Their headquarters at 69 Balliol Road and William James was the Scoutmaster. The group closed in 1952.
- Plans were prepared to create a 'Bootle Garden Village' consisting of 800 homes, on a 28-acre site near Ford Station, on land bought from the Earl of Sefton.
- Bootle Football Club was re-formed and played its first game at Stuart Road against Barnoldswick; the score was 1 - 1. The club manager was Walter Halsall, a former Marine and Blackburn Rovers player.
- Conversion from trams to buses began.
- Closure of the Strand Cinema, Irlam Road. The building was later used as a warehouse but was destroyed by fire in 1964.

B1354

29. Gladstone Dock
Smoke from the massive fire at Gladstone Dock, 1949, could be seen for miles.
(Photo courtesy Photoflex Studios)

1949

- The Bishop of Liverpool consecrated a temporary church for St Mary's parish in Queens Road on March 18th, following its amalgamation with the parish of St John.
- Princess Elizabeth and the Duke of Edinburgh visited the radar station at Gladstone Dock on March 22nd.
- On July 11th the Mayor opened new premises for the Bootle branch of the YMCA at 150-152 Stanley Road.
- The temporary branch library in Orrell was relocated to the grounds of the old fever hospital in Linacre Lane.
- The Mayor re-opened Bootle Museum, it having been closed for the duration of the war.
- Bootle built its first post-war house in Park Street; it was named 'The Cottage'.
- Re-opening of the ODVA (Orrell and District Veterans' Association) club in Fernhill Road. This building replaced the one destroyed in the 1941 Blitz.

- The Mayor unveiled a plaque in the Central Police Station in memory of the eight policemen killed during the war.
- William Keenan MP, for Kirkdale, performed the opening ceremony of the first phase of the Rimrose Brook Drainage Scheme on October 4th.
- A huge fire broke out at Gladstone Dock on November 9th. The Bootle Fire Brigade were at the scene within two minutes of the alarm being raised at South No. 2 Warehouse and were soon joined by neighbouring brigades. The ferocity of the fire resulted in a pall of black smoke hanging over Bootle all day.

1950

- Founding of the 23rd Aintree (later 23rd Bootle) Boy Scout Group on January 20th at St Oswald's C of E Church, Netherton. The GSM was Herbert Harrington.
- The Bishop of Liverpool consecrated a temporary church for St Leonard's parish on February 25th. The foundation stone from the original church was incorporated into the foundations of the new building.
- Founding in February of the 23rd Bootle Boy Scout group at St Joan of Arc RC Church. The GSM was Rev. Brian Foley. The Group closed in 1956.
- In April memorial tablets commemorating those that gave their lives in the Second World War were unveiled in King's Gardens.
- Field Marshall Viscount Montgomery visited Bootle in May to inspect the 40th (King's) Bootle Tank Regiment.
- Founding of the 24th Bootle Boy Scout Group at St Monica's RC Church in May. The GSM was Rev. O. P. Brady. The group closed in 1955.
- On October 9th the Bishop of Liverpool dedicated Sunset Home, the Church Army Home in Merton Road.
- The Bootle and Crosby District Ladies' Circle was established.
- Everton old stars (including Dixie Dean) played Liverpool Old Stars at Bootle Stadium.
- The Conservative Club in Pembroke Road (originally known as Beaconsfield Hall, later as Pembroke Hall and finally as County Hall), which had been badly damaged in the Blitz, was demolished.
- Work began near Ford Station on the construction of Bootle Garden Village.
- The International Harvester Company established a factory in Orrell Lane to assemble balers.
- The Rev. James William Roxburgh (later Bishop of Fulham) was inducted as Vicar of St Matthew's Church. He was known locally as 'The Dockers' Parson'

1951

- Founding in February of the 26th Bootle Boy Scout Group at Balliol Road Methodist Church. The GSM was Rev. T. Wilkinson. The Group closed in 1970.
- Founding of the 25th Bootle Boy Scout Troop at St Winefride's RC Church in March. The Scoutmaster was Thomas McLear. The group closed in 1960

- The Bootle Corporation Act, which incorporated the greater part of Netherton from Lancashire County into the Borough, was passed on April 1st.
- The census taken on April 8th showed the population of Bootle as 74,302.
- The Festival of Britain was celebrated between May 19th and 27th when street parties were held in many Bootle streets. A festival exhibition entitled 'Maritime Bootle' was held in Bootle Art Gallery from September 8th to October 27th.
- The Mayor opened the rebuilt Bootle Protestant Free Church, Trinity Road, in August
- The Welsh Congregational Church in Merton Road was re-opened in September having been bombed twice during the war.
- In September the foundation stone of the Welsh Calvinistic Methodist Church, Stanley Road, was laid.
- The Mayor formally opened Netherton Moss County Primary School on October 9th. The school buildings had been taken over earlier in the year from Lancashire County Council.
- Stanley Road Baptist Church re-opened on October 20th.
- The Bootle Women's Organisation Committee was formed. It consisted of representatives of 22 organisations.
- Intensive clearance of slum areas in Bootle began.
- Bootle Football Club moved from Stuart Road Stadium to Seaforth Stadium.
- Netherton (part-time) Branch Library was opened in the Parish Hall, Bridge Lane.

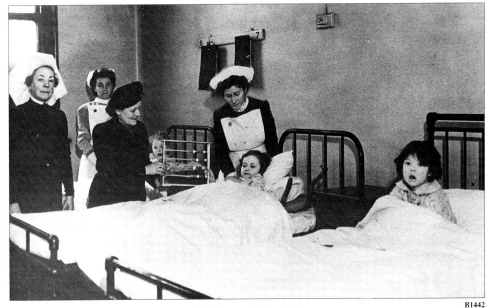

B1442

30. Borough Hospital
Presentation of gifts in the Children's Ward, Borough Hospital, 1950.

1952

- On February 5th the Mayor opened the new St John's C of E Primary School, built on the site of the bombed school.
- The Archbishop of Liverpool opened St Winefride's RC Junior Girls' School in Pembroke Road and the Boys' School in Merton Road on April 8th.
- Councillor H. Cullen, Chairman of the Baths Committee, opened the rebuilt Balliol Road Baths on April 30th.
- The Labour Party took control of Bootle Council in May, and Councillor Mark Connolly was elected Mayor.
- The last burial took place in St Mary's churchyard in July.
- Orrell Junior School was divided into two departments under separate Headteachers, Mr Hall (Boys) and Miss Moore (Girls).
- Mr E. Merion Evans laid the foundation stone for the Welsh Presbyterian Church, being rebuilt on the corner of Stanley and Trinity Roads.
- The Old Bootleians (Old Boys of Bootle Grammar School) presented their old school with a library table and two chairs as a memorial to ex-pupils and staff who gave their lives during the Second World War.

1953

- January 25th saw the loss of the 'Empress of Canada' by fire in the Gladstone Dock.
- There was a programme of events in Bootle from May 30th to June 12th to mark the Coronation of Queen Elizabeth II. A Coronation Carnival took place on June 27th.
- The Bootle & District Historical Society was founded on September 30th.
- Alderman Simon Mahon laid the foundation stone of the new Bootle Grammar School for Boys in Netherton on October 22nd.
- Building of the Rimrose Road housing estate began.
- Opening of Harmony Hall in Cinder Lane, Orrell, as the headquarters of the Orrell Women's Co-operative Guild.

1954

- Field Marshall Sir John Harding, Chief of the Imperial Staff, visited Bootle on April 11th to present new colours to the 40th (The King's) Royal Tank Regiment T.A.
- During renovation to the interior of Balliol Road Methodist Church in April a capsule was found buried deep in the Sunday School wall. It contained church papers, coins, newspapers dated 21st May 1889, and a programme describing the ceremony of the laying of the foundation stone. The renovation was completed in 1955 and it opened on March 20th, the only surviving Methodist Church in Bootle with services in English.
- The Mayor opened St George of England County Secondary School for Boys on July 20th. This was the first County Secondary School to be built since 1932. Mr Alec Fletcher, previously Headmaster of Robert's Boys' Secondary School, was appointed Headmaster.

- In August the Jehovah's Witnesses opened Kingdom Hall in Park Street.
- Knowsley Road Welsh Methodist Church was opened in August after war damage.
- The bomb-damaged Welsh Presbyterian Church on the corner of Stanley and Trinity Roads re-opened on September 23rd following rebuilding work. It was the first spired church to be built in Bootle for over 80 years.
- Queen Elizabeth II and the Duke of Edinburgh visited Bootle on October 21st – the first reigning queen, as monarch, to visit the borough.
- The Mayor opened Basil Grange Home for the Elderly in West Derby on November 15th. The house had been purchased the previous year from Dr M. Glynn.
- Work on the second phase of the Rimrose Brook Drainage Scheme was completed in December.
- A school crossing patrol service began in Bootle.
- The Mayor laid the foundation stone of Orrell Branch Library.
- A special ceremony was held to mark the completion of 13 Anderson Avenue – the 2,017th

B598

31. The Gas Board Showroom
The Gas Board Showroom in Stanley Road was built mid-1950s and demolished in late 1960s during re-development of the town centre. The Triad building now occupies the site.

house to be built following the end of the Second World War. This coincided with the number of houses destroyed during the war.
- Opening of the Bootle Citadel of the Salvation Army Corps in Stanley Road. In attendance was Mary Booth, granddaughter of General Booth, the Army's founder. In December the 27th Bootle Boy Scout Group was founded and met in the Citadel with Sydney Warne as GSM. The Group closed in 1957.
- The Archbishop of Liverpool consecrated St Alexander's RC Church in Brasenose Road on August 2nd. This replaced the church destroyed in the 1941 Blitz.

1955

- On January 10th a temporary school, to be known as Sterrix County Primary School, was opened in former army huts, close to the golf course in Sefton Moss Lane. Mrs A.H. Jones was appointed Headmistress.
- The Mayor opened Orrell Branch Library in Linacre Lane on September 14th.
- The Bishop of Liverpool opened St Leonard's new church hall on December 9th.
- The Bishop of Liverpool dedicated a new hall for the parish of St Mary.

1956

- An extension to Connolly House, Residential Home for the Blind, was opened on January 6th.
- The Gaumont Cinema in Stanley Road, with seating for 1,350 patrons, was opened on January 23rd, on the site of the bombed Broadway Cinema. The Mayor, in the presence of the actor Anthony Steel, performed the ceremony. The first film to be shown was 'Simon and Laura' starring Peter Finch and Kay Kendall. The cinema was closed on 1st November 1975: it is now known as Riley's.
- The Princess Royal opened the Princess Royal Primary School on February 29th. Miss A. D. Mills was appointed Headmistress. While in Bootle the Princess also opened the King George VI Social Club, Knowsley Road.
- Dave Rent of Bootle won the ABA Heavyweight Championship at Wembley in May.
- The automatic telephone exchange in Queens Road was opened on November 14th.
- The original Christ Church parish hall in Breeze Hill was sold to the YMCA for £9,500.
- The RC parish of Our Lady of Walsingham was established and for the next two years Mass was held in the canteen of the Metal Box Company in Leckwith Road. The first parish priest was Rev. Cornelius McEnroe.
- The foundation stone of St Winefride's RC Church, Oriel Road, was laid.
- Slum clearance in the Derby Road / Marsh Lane area began.
- Opening of St Monica's Catholic Young Men's Society social club in Stewart Avenue, in two former army huts.
- The foundation stone of Holy Ghost RC Church, Netherton, was laid.

1957

- The Mayor opened St Paul's Day Special School for pupils with learning difficulties in Menai Road on May 6th. Mr G.E. Newns was appointed Headmaster.
- Opening of the fountain in Morton Gardens in May. It was named in honour of the Mayoress, Mrs Bella Harris.
- Opening in May of S.J. Liggett Ltd's new self-service store at 35 Stanley Road.
- In May the 40th (The King's) Royal Tank Regiment was re-designated the Cadet Squadron 40/41st Royal Tank Regiment.
- The Mayor opened the Mount Hotel in Galsworthy Avenue, Orrell, in July.
- The Archbishop of Liverpool consecrated St Winefride's RC Church, Oriel Road, on September 15th. Built at a cost of £75,000 it seats 550. The organ from the earlier church was renovated and installed. The first parish priest in the new church was the Rev. J.J. McDowell. This replaced the church at the junction of Derby Road and Chapel Street, in the former Derby Road Baptist Chapel.
- Sir Edward Boyle, Parliamentary Secretary to the Minister of Education, opened Warwick Bolam County Secondary School on September 30th. It was named after Bootle's first Director of Education, and Mr D. Griffiths was appointed Headmaster.
- The process of converting the electric tram service to an all-bus system was completed in September.
- Peter Pell, credit tailoring, of 265 Stanley Road opened for business in November.
- The Earl of Derby opened new premises for Johnson's Cleaners and Dyers in Mildmay Road on November 27th. This replaced the buildings bombed in 1941.
- The C of E parish of St Oswald's, Netherton, was established. The Rev. Paul Turton was inducted as Vicar and served until 1964.
- Opening of the Park Hotel in Dunnings Bridge Road.

1958

- The Archbishop of Liverpool consecrated Holy Ghost RC Church, Netherton on May 28th.
- The Palace Cinema in Marsh Lane was closed on April 26th. The last film to be shown was 'The River of No Return'.
- In September Bootle took over responsibility for St Benet's RC Primary School, Sefton, from Lancashire Education Committee.
- The Mayor inaugurated the Mobile Library Service for Netherton in October.
- The C of E parish of St John's ceased to exist when it was divided between the parishes of Christ Church and St Mary's.
- Hawthorne Road Primary School closed due to falling rolls. Christ Church C of E Infant School moved into the vacated building.
- A wooden church for use by the RC parish of Our Lady of Walsingham was erected in Park Avenue. This building later became the parish hall.

- St Joan of Arc RC Church, Peel Road, was destroyed by fire.
- A tipstaff (truncheon), as used by Bootle's first police officers in 1840, was returned to the Borough.
- Mrs. E. Milne of Sydney, Australia, a relative of Mayor James Leslie (1884-5), returned to the Borough a trowel and mallet used during the foundation stone-laying ceremony of Bootle Library and Art Gallery on November 4th 1885. They are now on display in Bootle Town Hall.

B758

32. The Town Hall
The Town Hall, pictured here in 1958, suffered a hit in the Blitz;
the damage was not fully repaired until 1959-62.

1959

- The Imperial Cinema in Stanley Road closed on March 7th and was demolished in the late 1970s. The last film to be shown was 'Kings Go Forth'.
- Mr J. Cockbayne opened the Methodist Church, Gorsey Lane, in July.
- An agreement was reached between St Mary's Church authorities and Bootle Corporation that a Garden of Rest be created on the site of the original church.
- The Countess of Derby opened St Oswald's C of E Junior School on October 21st and the Bishop of Liverpool dedicated the building. This was the first post-war Primary School

built by Bootle. Godfrey Doubleday was appointed Headmaster.

- In November a roundabout replaced the traffic lights at the junction of Merton Road, Hawthorne Road, Breeze Hill and Oxford Road. It was dedicated to the memory of Alderman Mark Connolly. To enable this work to be carried out, a section of Christ Church churchyard was required. The church gave the land to Bootle Corporation in exchange for the upkeep of the churchyard in perpetuity.
- Plans were laid to construct a four-form entry RC secondary school (St Augustine's) in King Avenue, to cater for St Monica's and St Robert Bellarmine's parishes.
- Due to increasing numbers temporary classrooms were provided at St Benets RC Primary School.

1960

- Johnson Brothers donated a collection of paintings to Bootle Art Gallery in January.
- Official opening of the Countess of Derby County Secondary School for Girls in Browns Lane on March 17th by Princess Margaret, who was making her first visit to Bootle. Miss S. Stone was appointed as Headmistress.
- Official opening of the Bootle Social Centre for Children in Marsh Lane in March by the Earl of Derby. The building had previously housed the Palace Cinema.
- The Bishop of Liverpool laid the foundation stone of St Oswald's Church, Netherton, on April 30th.
- Alderman Hugh Baird opened Netherton Park County Junior School on May 24th.
- In August a decision was made to reduce the length of the school day for infant pupils. From September the afternoon session ended at 3.30 instead of 4pm.
- The Bishop of Liverpool opened Christ Church parish hall, Oxford Road, on September 9th.
- The Mayor opened Salisbury House in Marsh Lane on September 27th. This was Bootle's first eleven-storey block of flats.
- The Mayor officially opened Netherton Park County Infant School on October 4th. Miss M. Roberts was appointed Headmistress.
- The Gainsborough Cinema in Knowsley Road closed on November 12th and was converted into a bingo hall. The building was demolished in 2004.
- On December 17th Alderman Simon Mahon MP opened new premises for the Bootle Irish National Club in Derby Road.
- Christ Church Junior School ceased to use Eden Vale, a large house on the corner Hawthorne and Balliol Roads, as an annexe.
- The Corporation gave permission to the 12th Bootle Boy Scouts to erect a hut in Captain's Lane for their headquarters.

1961

- New Year's Honours: Albert Mills received the OBE for services to education and the Boy Scout Movement. Mr Mills was for many years Headmaster of Balliol Boys Secondary School and warden of Tawd Vale Scout Camping Ground near Ormskirk.
- Opening of St Luke's Junior Training Centre, Poulsom Drive, by Lord Cohen of Birkenhead on January 9th.
- Opening of the Marian Square shopping precinct on February 4th by the Mayor. A piece of modern sculpture entitled 'Growth and Development', donated by the London Development Company, was unveiled.
- The census taken on April 24th showed the population of Bootle as 82,773.
- The Archbishop of Liverpool consecrated St Joan of Arc RC Church on June 2nd.
- The Bishop of Liverpool consecrated St Oswald's C of E Church, Netherton, on September 16th.
- Opening of St Thomas Aquinas RC Secondary School for Boys in Swifts Lane, Netherton, on September 4th. Mr P. Hagan was appointed Headmaster.
- The Bishop of Liverpool consecrated a Garden of Rest in St Mary's churchyard, Irlam Road, on September 20th.
- On September 21St Lt. Gen. Sir William Stratton, Inspector General of Civil Defence, officially opened Goddard Hall in Knowsley Road as a Civil Defence HQ and demonstration theatre. It was built on the site of the former Cookson's Farm.
- In November Headteachers were given permission to introduce television into schools as a teaching aid. The full cost had to be met by the individual schools.
- The Rt Hon. John Hare officially opened the new Bootle Labour Exchange in Stanley Road. Previously it had been situated in the old Christ Church parish hall.
- Demolition of Church Street began as part of the slum clearance programme.
- The Appleby Flour Mills on the canal bank near Stanley Road Bridge were closed. They were demolished in 1965.
- Opening of the YMCA in the old Christ Church parish hall in Breeze Hill.
- Closure of St James' Secondary School for Boys.

1962

- In January the last group of pupils from Bootle Grammar School for Boys moved to new school premises in Netherton, thus finally vacating the Balliol Road site.
- The Mayor made telephone history in the town when he inaugurated the new subscriber trunk dialling (STD) telephone system by which subscribers were able to dial their own trunk calls. The first call was to Mr E.H. Lee, Mayor of Wembley.
- Alderman Peter Mahon, Chairman of the Finance Committee, re-opened the Town Hall on September 26th after extensive refurbishment.
- St Andrew's Memorial Hall, replacing the parish hall destroyed in 1941, opened.
- The Council agreed to allow Stuart Road Playing Fields to be used as an emergency landing ground for the RAF helicopter bringing patients to Walton and Fazakerley hospitals.
- St James' Junior boys and girls departments were amalgamated.

N /A

33. The junction of Merton Road and Hawthorne Road
The junction of Merton Road and Hawthorne Road viewed from Christ Church, shortly before the construction of the roundabout, 1959.
Lord Derby's hunting lodge (1773), No.1 Merton Road, is on the left.

34. Post-war Housing
The post-war housing shortage was met in the 1960s by new developments such as these flats in The Marian Way, Netherton.

B583

- Opening of Netherton Branch Library in Glover's Lane by the Mayor.
- Queen Elizabeth II and the Duke of Edinburgh visited Bootle to open the extension to Langton Dock.

1963

- A decision was taken to close Christ Church Mission Church, Waterworks Street. The mission had served the people of Bootle Village for almost 100 years.
- On October 10th a welfare centre and offices for parks and cemetery staff was opened in Linacre Lane, adjacent to Bootle Cemetery.
- The Bootle Times newspaper moved to new offices in Marsh Lane.

1964

- In January documents found in Mons, Belgium, included maps and photographs of Bootle used by German pilots on wartime bombing raids. A decision was taken to twin Bootle with Mons.
- Captain Walker's Old Boys' Association was formed in May.
- Alderman Peter Mahon opened new buildings for Bootle Grammar School for Boys in The Marian Way, Netherton, on May 4th. The Headmaster was Vincent Hayes.

- A delegation from Mons in Belgium visited Bootle in June for the first part of the twinning ceremony.
- St Augustine's RC Mixed Secondary School was opened in July with Mr G. O'Donnell as the Headmaster.
- The Salesian RC Grammar School for Boys was opened on September 8th in St Martin's College, Stanley Road. Five Brothers from the Salesian Order were appointed members of staff.
- In September Mater Misericoriae High School in Maghull, became a voluntary aided RC girls' grammar school, maintained by Bootle. (The school later became co-educational and was re-named Maricourt High School). The Headmistress was Sister Mary Magdalene.
- St Winefride's RC Girls' Secondary department closed in September. The pupils moved to St James' RC Girls' Secondary department.
- A delegation of councillors and officials from Bootle visited Mons in September for the final part of the twinning ceremony.
- A replica bell from HMS 'Starling', Captain Walker's ship, was presented to Bootle Council in October. The bell is rung to signify the start of Council meetings.
- The 7th Bootle Boy Scout Group moved from Ash Street Baptist Church and amalgamated with the 9th Bootle at St Andrew's Church.
- The Gaumont Cinema in Stanley Road was renamed The Odeon.

1965

- St Thomas Aquinas RC Mixed Secondary School was reorganised in January and became St Thomas Aquinas RC Boys' Secondary School. Pending the completion of the building of St Catherine's RC Girls' Secondary School in Copy Lane, Netherton, the girls had to share the St Thomas Aquinas site.
- The Archbishop of Liverpool laid the foundation stone of the Salesian High School, Netherton Way, on January 31st.
- On July 14th Denis Howells MP opened Netherton Youth Centre in the grounds of Warwick Bolam County Secondary School.
- Emmanuel Congregational Church in Stanley Road was destroyed by fire in July.
- Douglas Houghton MP, Chancellor of the Duchy of Lancaster, officially opened the Adult Training Centre for adults with learning difficulties in Dunnings Bridge Road on October 8th. Previously the adults had attended St Luke's Training Centre.
- The BBC broadcast a 'Songs of Praise' service from St James' RC Church.
- Opening of Worcester Road Youth Centre in premises previously occupied by the School Meals' Service.
- Opening of the Don Bosco Youth Centre in the Salesian College.
- Responding to Government Circular 10/65, Bootle made plans to re-organise secondary education in the Borough on comprehensive lines.
- Establishment of a regional office of George Wimpey & Co., Ltd. builders and civil engineers in Bridle Road, Netherton.

B802

35. Magdalen House
Magdalen House, one of many post-war office blocks, had a traditional 'Topping Out' ceremony in 1966 with Mayor Griffith Williams.

- Opening of the Liverpool Boys' Association Brunswick Boys' Club in Marsh Lane.

1966

- The Mayor opened The Mons public house at the corner of Balliol and Southport Roads on March 30th. It was named after Bootle's twin town in Belgium. (It is now known as The Hilltop.) Norfolk House, the family home of Alderman James Mack, earlier occupied the site.
- The 22nd Bootle Christ Church Boy Scout Group presented the Gang Show 'Wonderful Life' in Christ Church parish hall in April. More productions followed: It's a Great, Great Game (1967), Flying High (1968), Three Cheers (1969) We'll Go On and On (1971). Colin Sands produced them all.
- The Rt. Rev. Augustine Harris, Auxiliary Bishop of Liverpool, opened the Salesian College of St John Bosco RC Grammar School for Boys, Netherton Way, on September 15th. The Rev. Fr. A. Keogh was appointed Headmaster.
- The Standards of the 7th Battalion the King's (Liverpool) Regiment were laid up in Bootle Town Hall on October 22nd.
- The Council purchased, at a cost of £2,000, the Bishop Collection of Liverpool pottery from Mr G. Venmore Rowland.
- The Langton Hotel, which had stood on the corner of Strand and Stanley Roads since 1884 was demolished.
- St Winefride's presbytery in Merton Road was built.

1967

- In May Councillor Vera Bray was elected Mayor – the only woman to hold the office.
- The Minister for Housing and Local Government, Anthony Greenwood MP, officially opened Balliol House office block on May 26th.
- Interim arrangements for the introduction of comprehensive education in Bootle were introduced in September. The result was four comprehensive units catering for children from 11–16 and a sixth-form college for 16-18 year olds.
- Balliol Road Baths were re-opened on September 5th after modernisation.
- The Mayor opened Sterrix County Primary School on its new site in Daleacre Drive on October 31st
- St Winefride's Junior Boys' and Girls' Schools amalgamated and moved into the vacated Senior Boys' School, Merton Road. The senior boys were transferred to St Augustine's School. St Winefride's Infants transferred from Church View to Pembroke Road, into what had previously been the Junior Girls' School.
- The infant and junior departments of St Mary's School were amalgamated to form a JMI school with Mr William Rigby as Headmaster.
- Marsh Lane and Strand Road Station was renamed New Strand Station.
- Christ Church Mission Church, Waterworks Street, was demolished and the site was sold to Bootle Corporation.

- The Bootle and Liverpool police forces were amalgamated
- Bootle Justices were asked for the first time to deal with all matters arising in the Bootle dock system.

1968

- The Grange County Primary School and St Raymond's RC Primary School, Sefton, were taken over from Lancashire County Council in April.
- The new St Leonard's Church was consecrated on June 22nd.
- The first shop opened in the New Strand Shopping Centre on July 11th.
- From September Balliol Girls' and Boys' Secondary Schools were merged to create Balliol County Secondary Mixed School.
- Monsieur Leo Collard, Burgomaster of Mons, officially opened the first phase of the New Strand Shopping Centre on October 4th.
- The Archbishop of Liverpool opened St Catherine's RC Secondary School for Girls on October 17th. The Headmistress was Sister Rosario O'Malley.
- The Prime Minister Harold Wilson opened the National Girobank, Netherton Way, on October 18th.
- The centenary of Bootle as a municipality was marked by a special council meeting on December 30th at which a painting ('The Angel of Mons') by the Belgian artist Marcel Gillis was presented to the Borough. During the meeting Alderman Harry Oswald Cullen and Mrs Margaret Mahon were presented with illuminated scrolls in caskets when they were made Freemen of the Borough. A Civic Service at Christ Church, at which the preacher was the Bishop of Liverpool, the Rt Rev. Dr Stuart Blanche, followed this in the evening.
- St Monica's Junior Boys and Girls schools amalgamated on the Aintree Road site.
- The Mayor opened the Hoy-Carmel Recreation Centre at Cwm Penmachno in North Wales. Bootle Council bought the centre so that local youths in the care of the Probation Service could engage in outdoor activities.
- Bootle purchased further parts of Sefton.
- St George of England Secondary Modern School for Boys was amalgamated with Roberts' Girls School on the St George of England site.
- A Teachers' Centre for in-service training was established in Gray Street School. The first leader was Alec Fletcher who had recently retired as Headmaster of St George of England Secondary School for Boys.
- The redevelopment of Bootle Village began.
- The Mayor opened Stanley House in Marsh Lane
- Daniel House, a newly built office block in Stanley Road, was opened.

36. Street Party
In 1969 Bootle celebrated the centenary of the Borough Charter, granted December 1868.
This street party in Mary Road was one of many held to mark the event.
(Photo courtesy Bootle Times)

1969

- St Martin's House office block, Stanley Road, built on the site of St Martin's School, was opened in February.
- The Bishop of Liverpool opened new premises for St Mary's C of E Primary School in Browne Street on April 1st
- In May Bootle was awarded the Council of Europe Flag of Honour to mark the Borough's links with Europe. The flag is in the entrance to Bootle Town Hall.
- In July William L.S. Williams, American Consul-General, opened Washington Parade, behind New Strand Shopping Centre, to mark Bootle's close links with the USA
- The Orrell Hey Eventide Home for the Elderly in Orrell Road closed in August
- The Mayor opened Abbeyfield Park, in Park Lane, Netherton, and unveiled a memorial plaque in the pavilion on September 23rd.
- The Salem Welsh Congregational Church at the corner of Hawthorne Road and Breeze Hill was opened and dedicated on September 27th. Formerly in Merton Road, the church had been demolished in 1967. The congregation of the Welsh Baptist Church in Balliol Road joined them in the 1980s. The church finally closed in 1993 and the building became a private day nursery.
- Opening of the Mayflower Public House in the New Strand on October 1st by the Mayor. The name perpetuated a long association between Bootle and the USA
- Emmanuel Baptist Church in Fleetwood's Lane opened on October 18th. The church members were originally from Stanley Road Baptist Church, demolished in 1968.

- The Bootle Corporation Bill 1969 allowed the local authority to remove bodies from St Mary's churchyard in order to widen Derby Road.
- The Bootle boxer Johnny Cooke became British and Empire Welterweight champion.

1970

- Officers and ratings of the Sea Cadet Training Establishment HMS 'Stork' presented the ship's bell to Bootle Council in March.
- In June a house was purchased in Lytham St Annes as a holiday home for poor children from Bootle. The house had been an orphanage run by Anglican nuns.
- In September St Joan's RC Secondary School for Boys closed and the pupils were transferred to the Salesian College. The St Joan's building continued to be used for some time as an annexe.
- Dr Marie Clarke, for many years Deputy Medical Officer of Health for Bootle, opened the Marie Clarke Day Nursery in Linacre Lane on October 7th.
- Work began in November on the construction of the Triad, a 23-storey office block in Stanley Road. This is the tallest building in Bootle.
- A new building for St Benet's RC JMI School in Sefton was opened.
- The Bootle Schools' Music Group was established.

37. Mons Square
Mons Square, part of the massive New Strand Shopping Centre built on Stanley Road, late 1960s.

1971

- Bootle Hospital Outpatients' Department (the Robert Cox Memorial Building) in Derby Road closed in March.
- In April 70 acres of farmland in Sefton were earmarked for housing development.
- The census taken on April 25th showed the population of Bootle as 74,294.
- Skelly's car showroom in Linacre Lane opened in September. It relocated in 2005.
- Balliol Road Methodist Church closed on September 5th.
- Marks and Spencers opened their store in Stanley Road on November 4th.
- The Archbishop of Liverpool consecrated Our Lady of Walsingham RC Church, Netherton, in December
- Work began on building St John's House office block (between Merton and Trinity Roads) for use by the Inland Revenue. An industrial dispute that lasted on and off for seven years delayed its completion. The block was regarded by many who worked there as a 'sick building' and it was demolished in 2002.

1972

- Bootle Grammar School for Boys closed and the building was used to create a co-educational Sixth Form College for pupils from Bootle and Netherton schools.
- Linacre Park Presbyterian Church, Bailey Drive, celebrated its golden jubilee. Soon after, its congregation joined the United Reformed Church and renamed the church St Stephen's.
- St George of England Secondary School became a co-educational comprehensive school for pupils aged 11 –16. It was renamed St George of England High School.
- Opening of the Triad office block in Stanley Road.
- Bootle Hospital closed.
- Bootle Grammar School for Girls, Breeze Hill, amalgamated with Balliol Road Secondary Modern School. It was renamed Hillside High School and became a co-educational comprehensive school for pupils aged 11-16. David Terry was appointed Headmaster of the newly formed school.
- The Bootle Times newspaper moved its offices to the New Strand Shopping Centre.

1973

- In February number 32 Lunt Road was bought by the Corporation, renovated and refurbished as a show house to demonstrate what tenants could do with the help of grants.
- On May 5th the Mayor bestowed the Honorary Freedom of the Borough on the Plymouth Command of the Royal Navy. Three Royal Navy ships berthed at Bootle for the ceremony: HMS 'Plymouth', HMS 'Lincoln' and HMS 'Leopard'. Their ships' companies paraded through town past the saluting base, set up at the front of the New Strand shopping centre.
- A new peal of bells (from Emmanuel Church in Everton) was installed in Christ Church.

1974

- The Mayor opened Cambridge Road and Netherton Moss Nursery Schools on February 24th: each provided 40 places. Mrs G. Hurstfield was appointed Headmistress at Cambridge Road, and Mrs Eunice Connor at Netherton Moss.
- In February the Mayor opened Thomas Gray Infants School on land formerly occupied by Salisbury Road School. Mrs J.A. Seddon was appointed Headmistress.
- On March 9th the Freedom of the Borough was bestowed on Alderman Oliver Ellis, Councillor John Hevey, Councillor Simon Mahon MP, Councillor Margaret Frances Morley, Alderman Roger Rogerson, and the Town Clerk, Arthur Taylor.
- The fire brigades of Merseyside were amalgamated into a county-wide force and Bootle ceased to have its own brigade.
- In September the Rev Robert Dennis, Vicar of Christ Church, formally opened the new Christ Church JMI C of E School in Brookhill Road. Mr Ernest Pike was appointed Headmaster.
- Linacre Gas Works in Litherland Road closed.
- Marsh Lane Police Station opened. It replaced the former police station in Oriel Road.
- Alderman Hugh Baird opened Balliol Road Community Centre, in premises previously occupied by the Post Office, at the corner of Balliol and Oriel Roads.
- Opening of the School of the Good Shepherd on the site of Ford Convent in Sterrix Lane.
- Opening of the Hugh Baird College of Further Education by the Mayor. It is named after Hugh Baird, a former Chairman of the Education Committee.
- Orrell Junior and Infant Schools were amalgamated as Orrell County Primary School under the headship of Mr David Cheetham.
- From April 1st the County Borough of Bootle ceased to exist as a separate entity when it was incorporated into the newly formed Metropolitan District (later Borough) of Sefton.

N/A

38. The last Mayor William Wiseman
William Wiseman, last Mayor of Bootle. On April 1st 1974, local government reorganisation meant that Bootle became part of the new Metropolitan Borough of Sefton.

Some Major Developments in Bootle Since 1974

With local government reorganisation April 1st 1974 Bootle ceased to exist as a separate County Borough and became part of the Metropolitan District (later Borough) of Sefton that stretched from Bootle in the south to Southport in the north.

In 1979 a new library was built in Stanley Road. This enabled the old library, museum and art gallery buildings to be used for the Council's Education Department. The extensive museum and art gallery collections relocated to Southport and the local history archives to Crosby Library. On May 8th 1991, Princess Margaret opened the new Magistrates Courts in Merton Road.

Falling rolls in local schools brought about dramatic changes in the field of education. The first casualties were St. Catherine's and St Thomas Aquinas RC High Schools in Netherton, which were merged to form St. Ambrose Barlow RC High School (on the St Catherine's site) in 1981. Next to amalgamate were the Countess of Derby and Warwick Bolam High Schools, in Netherton, to form Bootle High School in 1984. Meanwhile St Paul's Special School closed in 1980. David Sheppard, Bishop of Liverpool, opened the newly refurbished and extended Hillside High School on May 9th 1989. The following year St. Augustine's and Salesian RC High Schools merged to form Savio High School - taking its name from St Dominic Savio the patron saint of schoolchildren.

There were many changes in the primary sector. The Princess Royal School fell victim to falling rolls and closed in 1990. The pupils of Bedford Road School moved to a brand new building in Balliol Road in 1992. In September 2005 St. Mary's C of E, St Winefride's with St. Richards RC, Daleacre and Netherton Park Schools closed. Roberts and Orrell Schools were amalgamated in 2006 to form Springwell Park School, built on the former St. Paul's School site in Menai Road.

The office-building boom of the 1960s has continued. Vermont House in Stanley Road opened in 1975. The Regional Health Authority moved into St Martin's House in 1982. The ill-fated St John's building in Merton Road built in 1971 was demolished in 2002 and replaced by a new building on the same site. The Health and Safety Executive that, in 1985 had moved into new office blocks (St. Hugh's, St. Peter's and Magdalen Houses) moved in 2006 into purpose-built premises in Pembroke Road. The Triad Building now houses, among other organisations, a department of the Inland Revenue.

Many changes have also taken place in community services. For example, in 1977 Age Concern opened a welfare centre in Marsh Lane. Three sheltered housing developments were undertaken: Bailey Court, Roberts Place (1978), Orrell Lodge, Rafter Avenue, opened by the Patrick Jenkins MP, Secretary of State for the Environment (1984) and Windsor Court, corner of Northfield and Windsor Roads (1986). Finally two community centres have been opened, Marsh Lane (1987) and Queens Road (1990).

Falling congregations have affected churches of all denominations. St. Paul & Trinity Presbyterian Church was demolished in 1981, except for the former manse. In the Anglican sector St. Mary's Church was never rebuilt on the original site but the Bishop of Warrington, the Rt. Rev. Michael Henshall, consecrated a worship centre in St. Mary's School on September 26th 1981. In 1983 St Oswald's Church, Netherton, fell victim to high alumina cement problems and subsequently had to be demolished. The parish took over the redundant infant school building and turned it into a worship centre. Finally in 2003 the Anglican parishes of St. Mary's, St. Andrew's, St. Matthew's and St. Leonard's were amalgamated. The 1980s saw a change of name for the R C parish of the Holy Ghost, Netherton, which became Holy Spirit. St. Alexander's RC church closed in 1991 and the parish was amalgamated with St. Richards'; this subsequently amalgamated with St. Monica's. Two points of church growth have occurred: the opening of a Youth and Community Centre at Christ Church in 1991, and a Community Centre in the former St. Monica's School buildings in Fernhill Road.

In 1980 P&O Ferries relocated their Belfast service to Brocklebank Dock, Bootle. That same year the Bootle and Southport police divisions of Merseyside Police were merged. Bootle Village was redeveloped, creating an attractive new centre to the district. A new health centre was opened in Park Street in 1983, and the old Knowsley Road Clinic was demolished and replaced by the May Logan Centre.

Recently Stanley Road, from Marsh Lane almost to the Liverpool boundary, has been redeveloped. The roads and pavements are completely resurfaced, new street furniture is in place and trees have been planted. The section that fronts the New Strand shopping centre is now subject to traffic restrictions that have created safer pedestrian areas in this very busy district. Bootle continues to grow and develop - and long may that continue.

MAYORS OF BOOTLE

Mayors elected in November until 1948 then elected in May.

Charles Howson	March - November 1869
William Geves	1869 - 1870
Thomas P. Danson	1870 - 1871
William Molyneux	1871 - 1873
William Geves	1873 - 1874
George Barnes	1874 - 1875
Thomas P. Danson	1875 - 1877
Louis W. Heintz	1877 - 1878
John Newell	1878 - 1879
John P. McArthur	1879 - 1880
William Poulsom	1880 - 1882
James Webster	1882 - 1884
James Leslie	1884 - 1885
Matthew Hill	1885 - 1886
William Jones	1886 - 1887
John Howerd	1887 - 1888
John Wells	1888 - 1889
Benjamin Cain	1889 - 1890
John Vickers	1890 - 1892
William Thomas	1892 - 1893
Benjamin S. Johnson	1893 - 1895
Isaac A. Mack	1895 - 1897
John McMurray	1897 - 1898
William R. Brewster	1898 - 1899
George Lamb	1899 - 1900
Peter Ascroft	1900 - 1901
George S. Wild	1901 - 1902
William H. Clemmey	1902 - 1903
James J. Metcalf	1903 - 1904
Owen K. Jones	1904 - 1905
Robert E. Roberts	1905 - 1906
Alfred Rutherford	1906 - 1907
James Pearson	1907 - 1908
George Randall	1908 - 1909
Hugh Carruthers	1909 - 1910
James R. Barbour	1910 - 1911
John W. E. Smith	1911 - 1912
William H. Clemmey	1912 - 1913
John Rafter	1913 - 1914
George A. Cassady	1914 - 1915
James Pearson	1915 - 1916
Benjamin E. Bailey	1916 - 1917
James Pearson	1917 - 1918
Harry Pennington	1918 - 1920
John H. Johnston	1920 - 1922
Thomas A. Patrick	1922 - 1923
Robert Turner	1923 - 1924
Birty Wolfenden	1924 - 1925
Thomas Harris	1925 - 1926
Frederick W. King	1926 - 1927
Edmund Gardner	1927 - 1929
Simon Mahon	1929 - 1930
Donald S. Eaton	1930 - 1931
Arthur Hankey	1931 - 1932
James Scott	1932 - 1933
Maurice S. Webster	1933 - 1934
Edwin Smith	1934 - 1935
John W. Clark	1935 - 1936
James Burnie	1936 - 1937
James O'Neill	1937 - 1938
Nicholas Cullen	1938 - 1939
James Spence	1939 - 1940
Joseph S. Kelly	1940 - 1941
Joseph S. Riley	1941 - 1942
Richard O. Jones	1942 - 1943
George A. Rogers	1943 - 1944
William Keenan	1944 - 1945
John T. Hackett	1945 - 1946
Harry O. Cullen	1946 - 1947
Thomas Harris	1947 - 1949
George G. Anderson	1949 - 1950
David B. Black	1950 - 1951
Robert J. Rogerson	1951 - 1952
Mark Connolly	1952 - 1953
Robert J. Rainford	1953 - 1954
Peter Mahon	1954 - 1955
Thomas A. Cain	1955 - 1956
Israel Harris	1956 - 1957
Albert S. Moore	1957 - 1958
John C. Hevey	1958 - 1959
Hugh Baird	1959 - 1960
Joseph S. Kelly	1960 - 1961
Joseph S. Kelly	1961 - 1962
Simon Mahon (Junior)	1962 - 1963
Joseph Morley	1963 - 1964
Thomas Dooley	1964 - 1965
Griffith Williams	1965 - 1966
James Grimley	1966 - 1967
Vera Bray	1967 - 1968
Oliver Ellis	1968 - 1969
Harold Gee	1969 - 1970
Fredrick Morris	1970 - 1971
George Halliwell	1971 - 1972
John Marray	1972 - 1973
William Wiseman	1973 - 1974

CHIEF CONSTABLES

Captain Arrowsmith	1887 - 1888
Mr. Adrian D'Espiney	1888 - 1891
Mr. James Cummings	1891 - 1905
Mr. John Stewart	1905 - 1918
Major W. D. Allen	1918 - 1920
Mr. Philip Theodore Briarley Browne	1920 - 1926
Mr. Thomas Bell	1926 - 1949
Mr. William E. Pitts	1949 - 1953
Mr. Harold E. Legge	1953 - 1967
Mr. James Houghton (Liverpool & Bootle)	1967 - 1974

TOWN CLERKS OF BOOTLE

Mr. Richard Holden ....1869 - 1870
Mr. Thomas Draper Pierce.......................1870 - 1883
Mr. J. Henry Farmer ....1883 - 1914
Mr. J. Spencer Tumilty ....1914 - 1931
Mr. Harold Partington ....1931 - 1963
Mr. Arthur Taylor ....1963 - 1974

BOOTLE MEDICAL OFFICERS OF HEALTH

Dr. Robert John Sprakeling ....1873 - 1900
Dr. T. W. Naylor Barlow ....1900 - 1908
Dr. William Daley ....1908 - 1911
Sir William Allen Daley...........................1911 - 1921
Dr. F.T.H. Wood ....1921 - 1948
Dr. James Fairley Swan ....1948 - 1950
Dr. T. R. Roberton..................................1951 - 1964
Dr. G. T. MacCulloch ....1964 - 1974

BOOTLE CLERKS TO THE JUSTICES

Mr. Edward Cotton ....1877 - 1890
Mr. Edward L. Lewes ....1890 - 1910
Mr. Hadrian Sandiford.............................1910 - 1934
Mr. H.A.G. Langton.................................1934 - 1948
Mr. Percy Hulme......................................1948 - 1962
Mr. Frank Preston ....1963 - 1974

SOUTH SEFTON CLERKS TO THE JUSTICES

Mr. Frank Preston ....1974 - 1976
Mr. Charles Hughes ....1976 - 1990
Mr. Edward Platt (acting) ....1990 - 1991
Mr. Dennis Luty.......................................1991 - 1999
Mrs. Susan Bouche ....1999 -

MEMBERS OF PARLIAMENT

Col. Thomas Myles Sandys ....1885 - 1911
Mr. Andrew Bonar Law ....1911 - 1918
Sir Thomas Royden ....1918 - 1922
Major James Burnie M.C...........................1922 - 1924
Lt. Col. Vivian Leonard Henderson...........1924 - 1929
Mr. John Kinley ....1929 - 1931
Col. Chichester de Windt Crookshank ....1931 - 1935
Sir Eric Errington.....................................1935 - 1945
Mr. John Kinley ....1945 - 1955
Mr. Simon Mahon ....1955 - 1979
Mr. Alan Roberts......................................1979 - 1990
Mr. Michael Carr ....1990 - 1990
Mr. Joseph Benton ....1990 -

THE EARLS OF DERBY: BOOTLE'S MAJOR LANDOWNER

13th Earl Edward Smith Stanley ....1775 - 1851
14th Earl Edward George Geoffrey Smith Stanley...1851 - 1869
15th Earl Edward Henry Stanley ....1869 - 1893
16th Earl Fredrick Arthur Stanley ....1893 - 1908
17th Earl Edward George Villiers Stanley ....1908 - 1948
18th Earl Edward John Stanley ....1948 - 1994
19th Earl Edward Richard William Stanley ....1994 -

MAY QUEENS

Alice Parry... 1896
Jessie Clark.. 1897
Helena Hull Pringle 1898
Margaret Lowe 1899
Ethel Eaton 1900
Annie Griffiths 1901
Margaret Regan 1902
Christine Hamilton 1903
Elsie Fisher 1904
Miss Wolfenden.................................. 1905
Ruth Sanders 1906
Kathleen Miller 1907
Mary Agnes Dunne 1908
Isabella Rose 1909
Mabel Thomas.................................... 1910
Violet Wilson 1911
Christina McDonald 1912
Ella Phipps 1913
Janet Lamb 1914
War Years 1915-18
Jessie Coleman 1919
Lettie Wharton................................... 1920
Florence Hamilton 1921
Viola Carr.. 1922
Norah Collings 1923
Jean Pilkington 1924
Dorothy Spencer................................. 1925
Mary Mills... 1926
Pauline West Sadler............................ 1927
Phylis Spence 1928
Phylis Spence 1929
Bertha Prince 1930
Edna May Fairweather 1931
Mary Potter....................................... 1932
Dorothy McEwan 1933
Marjorie Roscoe 1934
Winifred Dunne 1935
Coralie Crocket 1936
Gladys Marshall 1937
Nina Mills.. 1938
Jean McKenzie 1939
Diana Mills.. 1940
War Years 1941-44

CARNIVAL QUEENS

Marjorie Jay	1945
Dorothy Higham	1946
Beryl Gibbs	1947
Beryl Jones	1948
Judith Daniels	1949
Caroline Baker	1950
Iris Forshaw	1951
Maureen Turner	1952
Margaret Wagner	1953
Joan Valerie Bullen	1954
Barbara Allan	1955
Patricia Vera Byrne	1956
Patricia Buckley	1957
Brenda Hannaway	1958
Brenda Hughes	1959
Pauline Keegan	1960
Doris Slowey	1961
Susan Allen	1962
Jane Owen	1963
	1964
Christine Edwards	1965
Lydia Jones	1966

CHIEF LIBRARIANS

Mr. John J. Ogle	1887 - 1901
Mr. Charles Henry Hunt	1901 - 1929
Mr. R.W. Lynn	1929 - 1934
Mr. Benjamin Robinson	1934 - 1950
Mr. Arthur Ritson Hardman	1950 - 1974

CHIEF FIRE OFFICERS

Mr. G. W. Parker	1886 -1892
(Resigned to command Belfast Fire Brigade)	
Mr. Henry Roberts	1892 - 1904
Mr. John Frederick Collins	1904 - 1915

Mr. J. Cole	1915 - 1926
Mr. James Cecil Monk	1926 - 1927
(Killed on duty)	
Mr. J. Cole	1927 - 1927
(Recalled from retirement until successor appointed)	
Mr. John Smith	1927 - 1931
(Resigned to command Belfast Fire Brigade)	
Mr. John Frederick Collins	1931 - 1941
(Son of former Chief Officer)	
National Fire Service	1941 - 1948
Mr. A J. Greenslade M.B.E.	1948 - 1954
Mr. R.K. Barlow M.B.E.	1954 - 1970

BOROUGH (ACCOUNTANTS) TREASURERS

Mr. George Craig	1885 - 1905
Mr. G. Bamford	1905 - 1907
Mr. J. Clark Nicol	1907 - 1914
Mr. Joseph Gronow	1914 - 1933
Mr. Daniel Williams	1933 - 1946
Mr. Lewis Wilson	1946 - 1965
Mr. Stephen Tyson	1965 - 1973
Mr. W. Hallatt	1973 - 1974

MATRONS OF BOOTLE HOSPITAL

Miss M. A. Irvine	1872 - 1876
Miss E. Lawton	1876 - 1881
Miss Getty	1881 - 1886
Miss Peck	1886 - 1888
Miss McDonald	1888 - 1891
Mrs. A. Roberts	1891 - 1917
Miss R. Jackson	1917 - 1936
Miss Annie Watts	1936 - 1950
Miss Marie Mountfield	1950 - 1967
Mrs. Edith Maggs	1967 - 1970
Miss Irene Vernon	1970 - 1974

BOROUGH SURVEYORS / ENGINEERS

Mr. John Alexander	1880 - 1890
Mr. W. N. Blair	1890 - 1894
Mr. J. A. Crowther	1894 - 1903
Mr. R. J. Wolfenden	1903 - 1932
Mr. William Arthur Harrison	1932 - 1956
Mr. Derek Taylor Bradshaw	1956 - 1960
Mr. Thomas William Crookdake	1960 - 1974

REGISTRARS

Mr. W. T. Johnson	1900 - 1925
	1925 - 1938
Mr. Sydney Wood	1938 - 1963
Mr. Norman Tudor	1963 - 1974

SECRETARIES / DIRECTORS OF EDUCATION

Mr. F. K. Wilson	1886 - 1920
Mr. Samuel Clarke	1920 - 1934
Mr. Warwick Bolam	1935 - 1958
Mr. William Richard John Coe	1958 - 1974

HEADTEACHERS OF BOOTLE SCHOOLS

■ **BEDFORD ROAD BOARD SCHOOL 1885, COUNCIL from 1903**

BEDFORD ROAD SENIOR BOYS DEPARTMENT

Mr. Austin John Miles	1885 - 1922

BEDFORD ROAD SENIOR GIRLS DEPARTMENT

Miss S. J. Lace	1885 - 1899
Miss Isabella Underwood	1899 - 1917
Miss E. E. Green	1917 - 1923

BEDFORD ROAD MIXED JUNIOR DEPARTMENT
Miss S. Forshaw.............................1886 - 1905

Miss Agnes Armstrong ....1905 - 1922

BEDFORD ROAD BOYS ALL AGE DEPARTMENT
Mr. Austin John Miles ....1922 - 1923

BEDFORD ROAD MIXED ALL AGE DEPARTMENT
Mr. Samuel Donaldson ....1923 - 1930

Seniors move to Balliol Secondary in 1930; Juniors and Infants from Balliol move to Bedford Road in 1934.

BEDFORD ROAD JUNIOR BOYS DEPARTMENT from 1930
Mr. Samuel Donaldson ....1930 - 1937

Mr. W. A. Blanchard ....1937 - 1958

BEDFORD ROAD JUNIOR GIRLS DEPARTMENT from 1930
Miss E. E. Green...............................1930 - 1940

Miss F. M. Bailey TIC ....1940 - 1947

Miss C. C. Pearson ....1947 - 1958

1958 Junior Boys' and Girls' departments amalgamate.

BEDFORD ROAD JUNIOR MIXED DEPARTMENT
Miss C. C. Pearson ....1958 - 1969

Mr. Gordon Knowles ....1969 - 1992

BEDFORD ROAD INFANTS DEPARTMENT
Miss Agnes Armstrong ....1885 - 1905

Miss Roberta Tate ....1905 - 1932

Miss E. Pritchard ....1932 - 1938

Miss F. Kay......................................1938 - 1942

Miss M.J. Hibbert ....1942 - 1964

Miss Ratcliffe(acting) ....1964 - 1965

Miss H.M. Shaw (died in post)...........1965 - 1966

Miss E.L. Peers ....1966 - 1969

Miss Joan Lunt................................1969 - 1992

Bedford Infant and Junior Departments amalgamate and move to new site in Balliol Road.

BEDFORD ROAD J.M.I. SCHOOL from 1992
Miss Joan Lunt................................1992 - 1994

Mr. Ian Chapman ....1994 - 2002

Mr. Gerald Ashley.............................2002 -

■ MUNICIPAL INTERMEDIATE DAY SCHOOL 1900
Boys' Secondary School from 1926: Grammar School for Boys from 1946

Mr. Frederick Gorse ....1901 - 1912

Mr. William Ditchburn........................1912 - 1926

BOOTLE BOYS' SECONDARY SCHOOL from 1926
Mr. William Ditchburn........................1926 - 1936

Mr. John D. Berbiers.........................1936 - 1946

BOOTLE GRAMMAR SCHOOL FOR BOYS from 1946
Mr. John D. Berbiers.........................1946 - 1961

Mr. Vincent Hayes ....1961 - 1972

WARWICK BOLAM SECONDARY MODERN MIXED SCHOOL 1954-9
Mr. D. Griffiths ....1957 - 1959

Boys remain at Warwick Bolam, girls move to newly opened Countess of Derby 1959

WARWICK BOLAM BOYS' SECONDARY MODERN SCHOOL 1959-73
Mr. D. Griffiths ....1959 - 1973

COUNTESS OF DERBY GIRLS' SECONDARY MODERN SCHOOL 1959-71
Miss S. Stone ....1959 - 1966

Mrs. S. Griffiths ....1966 - 1972

COUNTESS OF DERBY MIXED HIGH SCHOOL 1972-84
Mr. John Denham..............................1972 - 1980

Mr. Barry Gratton ....1980 - 1984

Warwick Bolam merges with Bootle Grammar School for Boys to create Warwick Bolam High School on Grammar School site, plus a Sixth Form College for all Bootle pupils. The Grammar School pupils remain and work their way through the school.

WARWICK BOLAM HIGH SCHOOL & SIXTH FORM COLLEGE 1973
Mr. Eric Macdonald ....1973 - 1983

Mr. Peter Middleton ....1983 - 1984

Warwick Bolam and Countess of Derby High Schools merge on the Countess of Derby site in 1984 to form Bootle High School.

BOOTLE HIGH SCHOOL
Peter Middleton...............................1984 - 1992

Caroline Sweeney ....1992 - 2002

Philip Fryer ....2002 -

■ BOOTLE SECONDARY SCHOOL FOR GIRLS from 1910
Miss Lydia Taylor ....1910 - 1925

Miss E.M. Steuart ....1925 - 1946

BOOTLE GRAMMAR SCHOOL FOR GIRLS from 1946
Miss Ethel M. Steuart ....1946 - 1950

Miss D.V. Blythe ....1950 - 1968
Miss J.P. Whitley ....1968 - 1972

■ BALLIOL ROAD COUNCIL SCHOOL 1914

BALLIOL ROAD SENIOR BOYS' DEPARTMENT
Mr. W.F. Towndrow ....1914 - 1932

BALLIOL ROAD SENIOR GIRLS' DEPARTMENT
Miss A. Peake ....1914 - 1932

In 1930 Bedford Senior pupils move to Balliol; girls' and boys' departments amalgamate in 1932

BALLIOL ROAD SENIOR MIXED DEPARTMENT
Mr. Albert Mills ....1932 - 1934

BALLIOL ROAD BOYS' SECONDARY MODERN from 1946
Mr. Albert Mills ....1934 - 1956
Mr. Stuart Elliot ....1956 - 1968

BALLIOL ROAD GIRLS' SECONDARY MODERN from 1946
Miss M. Stephens................................1934 - 1954
Miss M. A Weir ....1955 - 1958
Miss Stella Evans.................................1959 - 1968

The girls' and boys' departments amalgamate in 1968

BALLIOL ROAD MIXED SECONDARY MODERN SCHOOL
Mr. Stuart Elliot ....1968 - 1972

BALLIOL MIXED JUNIORS AND INFANTS DEPARTMENT
Miss E. Kay ....1914 - 1930
Miss E. Pritchard ....1931 - 1932

Miss M. Stephens................................1932 - 1934

Junior and Infant children move to Bedford Road Council School in 1934. In 1972 The Girls' Grammar School and Balliol County Secondary Schools merge to form a Comprehensive School, Hillside High School, catering for pupils aged 11-15. The Grammar School children remain in the school and work their way through.

HILLSIDE HIGH SCHOOL 1972
Mr. David Terry ....1972 - 1974
Mr. Don Duckworth............................1974 - 1990
Mrs. Collette McDonald ....1990 - 1995
Mr. John Neilly (acting)......................1995 - 1996
Mrs. L. C. R. Shemilt ....1996 -

■ CHRIST CHURCH NATIONAL SCHOOL 1866

CHRIST CHURCH BOYS' DEPARTMENT
Mr. T. Parkinson................................1866 - 1871
Mr. Stephen Hale ....1871 - 1900
Mr. A.E. Scott ....1900 - 1924
Mr. Henry H. Johnson........................1924 - 1930

In 1930 senior boys move to St. Mary's School and Christ Church Boys' becomes Junior Boys only.

CHRIST CHURCH GIRLS' DEPARTMENT
Miss Ellen Hawthorne ....1866 - 1881
Miss S.A. Finn ....1881 - 1905
Miss M.E. Boughey ....1905 - 1930

In 1930 Senior Girls from St. Mary's and St. John's Schools come to Christ Church.

Miss M. E. Boughey ....1930 - 1935
Miss Thompson (Teacher in Charge) .....1935 - 1936
Mrs Jessie Atkinson ....1936 - 1938

In 1938 the Senior Girls transfer to Balliol Secondary School. Christ Church becomes a Primary School.

CHRIST CHURCH JUNIOR BOYS' DEPARTMENT
Mr. Henry H. Johnson........................1930 - 1942

CHRIST CHURCH JUNIOR MIXED DEPARTMENT
Mr. Henry Johnson (died 12.11.64) .....1942 - 1949
Mr. Arnold Blackburn ....1949 - 1953
Mr. Ernest Pike ....1954 - 1974

CHRIST CHURCH INFANTS' DEPARTMENT
Miss Margaret Brades.........................1866 - 1881
Miss A. Bootle ....1880 - 1889
Miss A.J. Roberts ....1899 - 1923
Miss Mary E. Dougherty ....1923 - 1948
Miss Ethel Roberts.............................1948 - 1966
Miss E. M. I. Munroe (acting)..............1967 - 1967
Miss Jean Rawlinson ....1967 - 1974

In 1974 Junior and Infant departments amalgamate to form a J.M.I. School. School moves to new site (Brookhill Road)

CHRIST CHURCH J.M.I SCHOOL 1974
Mr. Ernest Pike ....1974 - 1976
Mr. James Welch ....1976 - 1997
Mr. Grahame L. Watts.........................1997 -

■ DAY INDUSTRIAL SCHOOL MARSH LANE 1898
Superintendents
Miss Phobe Wall ....1898 - 1906
Miss Sarah Ratchford ....1906 - 1913

■ SCHOOL OF THE GOOD SHEPHERD 1973
For Physically Handicapped and Delicate Children
Mr. C. K. Bell ....1973 - 1986

Mr. Alan M. Sullivan ....1986 - 2005

School closes 2005 and pupils transfer to Rowan Park School, Crosby.

■ GRAY STREET BOARD SCHOOL 1899, COUNCIL 1903

GRAY STREET BOYS' DEPARTMENT
Mr. William Milroy...1899 - 1910
Mr. Robert Raby ....1910 - 1927
Mr. E. J. Pengelly.....................................1927 - 1930
D.H. Whitehead ....1931 - 1942
J.Dixon ....1942 - 1946

GRAY STREET GIRLS' DEPARTMENT
Miss Kate Tatton ....1899 - 1900
Miss L. Laybourne ....1901 - 1930
Miss E. J. Keates....................................1931 - 1946

Senior pupils move to the old Nurses' Home buildings on the Linacre Hospital site. In 1953 boys move to St. George of England Secondary Modern Boys' School and girls to Roberts Secondary Modern Girls' School.

GRAY STREET MIXED SECONDARY MODERN SCHOOL 1946 - 1953
Mr. J. S. Williams ....1946 - 1952
Mr. E. Pike (temp i/c Senior Boys) ....1952 - 1953

GRAY STREET JUNIOR MIXED DEPARTMENT
Mr. R. Murray ....1946 - 1951
Mr. Evan Williams ....1951 - 1960
Mr. John Horn ....1960 - 1972

GRAY STREET INFANTS' DEPARTMENT
Miss Emma Paterson ....1899 - 1927
Mrs. Ada L. Morgan ....1927 - 1950

Miss A. H. Porterhouse ....1950 - 1954

In 1954 Infants move to Salisbury Road Infant School. In 1972 Gray Street and Salisbury Road schools amalgamate in new buildings on Salisbury Road site. Part of old Gray Street building used as Bootle's first Teachers' Centre.

THOMAS GRAY INFANTS' SCHOOL
Mrs. J. L. Seddon.....................................1972 - 1983
Miss Elizabeth Kent.................................1983 - 1989
Mrs. Margaret Lawrence nee Kelly ....1989 - 1990
Mrs. Eileen F. Walsh ....1990 - 2004

THOMAS GRAY JUNIOR SCHOOL
Mr. John Horn...1972 - 1983
Mr. R. J. Potter......................................1983 - 2004

THOMAS GRAY J.M.I. SCHOOL from 2004
Mr. R. J. Potter.....................................2004 -

■ HAWTHORNE ROAD. BOARD SCHOOL 1895, COUNCIL 1903

HAWTHORNE ROAD BOYS' DEPARTMENT
Mr. J.H.J. Stringer...................................1895 - 1923
Mr. Thomas A. Turton ....1923 - 1934

HAWTHORNE ROAD GIRLS' DEPARTMENT
Miss Emma Taylor (died in post) ....1895 - 1900
Miss Ida Robb..1900 - 1914
Miss Elizabeth Logan ....1914 - 1940
Miss A.B. Murphy ....1925 - 1934

Senior pupils move to Balliol School in 1934

HAWTHORNE ROAD JUNIOR BOYS from 1934
Mr. E. Preston ....1934 - 1941

HAWTHORNE ROAD JUNIOR GIRLS from 1934
Miss A. B. Murphy ....1934 - 1941

HAWTHORNE ROAD INFANTS' DEPARTMENT
Miss Ellen Forshaw ....1894 - 1926
Miss Annie Filshie ....1926 - 1941

Infant and Junior departments amalgamate in 1941

HAWTHORNE ROAD J.M.I. SCHOOL 1941-1958
Miss K. Parker ....1941 - 1958

■ HOLY GHOST (later HOLY SPIRIT) ROMAN CATHOLIC SCHOOL 1956

HOLY GHOST JUNIOR DEPARTMENT
Mr. John McElroy.....................................1956 - 1969

HOLY GHOST INFANT DEPARTMENT
Miss A. Geraghty ....1956 - 1965
Miss M. Fyles ....1965 - 1969

The Infant and Junior departments amalgamate in 1969

HOLY GHOST J.M.I. SCHOOL
Mr. Joe Coen ....1969 - 1986
Sister Mary McMahon ....1986 - 1993
Mr. Peter O'Brien ....1993 - 2004
Mr. Paul Davenport...................................2004 -

HOLY GHOST ANNEXE in Sterrix Lane 1957
Mr. B. Dwyer t. i. c. of Juniors in annexe ....1957 - 1960

■ KNOWSLEY ROAD BOARD SCHOOL 1892-1899
(Held in the Bootle Institute)
Mrs. Eberth ....1892 - 1895

Miss Matilda Stannard ....1895 - 1897

Miss C. E. Tanner ....1897 - 1899

■ LINACRE COUNCIL SCHOOL 1905

LINACRE BOYS' DEPARTMENT 1905 - 1939

Mr. A Yates ....1905 - 1929

Mr. John R. Dickinson ....1929 - 1939

LINACRE GIRLS' DEPARTMENT 1905 - 1939

G. Morrison.....................................1905 - 1933

Miss A Peake ....1933 - 1936

Miss Annie Griffiths ....1936 - 1939

*In 1939 senior children move to Gray Street or Balliol
Road Schools and Linacre becomes a Primary School*

LINACRE JUNIOR BOYS' DEPARTMENT

Mr. John R. Dickinson ....1939 - 1945

Mr. J. Spence...................................1945 - 1950

LINACRE JUNIOR GIRLS' DEPARTMENT

Miss Annie Griffiths ....1939 - 1943

Miss A. Marks...................................1943 - 1945

Miss E. M. Smyth ....1945 - 1950

In 1950 the Junior departments amalgamate

LINACRE JUNIOR MIXED DEPARTMENT

Mr. J. Spence ....1950 - 1960

LINACRE INFANT DEPARTMENT

Miss Florence E. Deyes ....1905 - 1932

Miss R. Tate ....1932 - 1935

Miss Mary McPherson.............................1935 - 1950

Miss I Spence...................................1950 - 1960

LINACRE J.M.I. SCHOOL from 1960

Mr. J. Spence...................................1960 - 1967

Mrs. E. Miller ....1967 - 1970

Mr. Charles Green...............................1970 - 1984

Mr. Michael Billing ....1984 - 1992

Mrs. Gill M. Hudson.............................1992 - 1998

Mrs. Barbara Yates ....1998 - 2004

Mss. Elaine Haney ....2004 -

MATER MISERICORIAE ROMAN CATHOLIC GRAMMAR SCHOOL FOR GIRLS, MAGHULL

From 1964 R. C. Girls from Bootle attend the school.

Sister Mary Magdalene (Miss J. P. Hardman)....1964 - 1967

In 1967 the school reorganises on comprehensive lines.

MARICOURT HIGH SCHOOL, MAGHULL

Sister Mary Magdalene (Miss J. P. Hardman)....1967 - 1990

Sister Mary Teresa (Miss Teresa McCarthy) ....1990 -

■ NETHERTON MOSS JMI SCHOOL 1951

Mr. Jack Lord ....1951 - 1954

In 1954 divides into Infant and Junior departments

NETHERTON MOSS JUNIOR DEPARTMENT 1954

Mr. Jack Lord...................................1954 - 1955

NETHERTON MOSS INFANT DEPARTMENT 1954

Mrs. D. Harewood ....1954 - 1955

*In 1955 due to increasing numbers the Infant and Junior
departments are split in half to produce 2 Infant and 2
Junior departments. The Junior departments are
accommodated in the new Grammar School for Boys; the
Infant departments in newly-opened Infant building and in
Junior building.*

NETHERTON MOSS (MAIN)

Mr. Jack Lord..................................1955 - 1959

*In 1959 Mr. Lord moves to newly-opened Netherton Park
JMI School, Park Lane with the children living in that area.*

NETHERTON MOSS (A)

Mr. B. T. Scott (temp).........................1955 - 1956

Mr. J. B. McDonald.............................1956 - 1972

(previously Headmaster of Netherton village school)

Mr. Peter Whiston.............................1972 - 1978

NETHERTON MOSS INFANTS MAIN

Mrs D. Harewood ....1951 - 1963

Miss H. J. Hibbert...........................1963 - 1978

Infants and Juniors amalgamate in 1978

NETHERTON MOSS J.M.I. SCHOOL from 1978

Mr. Colin Miller.............................1978 - 1996

Mrs. Susan Scott.............................1996

NETHERTON MOSS INFANTS 'A'

Miss Barbara Edwards.........................1951 - 1960

*In 1960 Miss Edwards and children living near newly-built
St. Oswald's County Infant School move to St. Oswald's to
create a new school.*

A Nursery School added to the Netherton Moss site 1974.

NURSERY

Mrs. Eunice Connor...........................1974 - 1987

■ NETHERTON PARK J. M. I SCHOOL 1959

Mr. Jack Lord................................1959 - 1960

In 1960 Netherton Park Infant School opens and the J. M.

I. School becomes a Junior School.

NETHERTON PARK JUNIOR SCHOOL
Mr. Jack Lord..1960 - 1972
Mr. Norman Connolly...1972 - 1987

NETHERTON PARK INFANTS' SCHOOL
Miss M. Roberts...1960 - 1972
Mrs. Val Ashton ....1972 - 1987

NETHERTON PARK J.M.I. SCHOOL
Mrs Val Ashton ....1987 - 1992
Mr. Michael S. Lumb ....1992 - 1997
Mrs. J. Aspinwall ....1997 - 2005

■ ORRELL COUNCIL SCHOOL 1910

ORRELL COUNCIL SCHOOL BOYS' DEPARTMENT
Mr. A. Philipson..1910 - 1931
Mr. Robert T. Robinson ....1931 - 1932
Mr. Charles F. Parkinson ....1932 - 1945
Mr. G.C.O. Hall ....1947 - 1947

ORRELL COUNCIL SCHOOL GIRLS' DEPARTMENT
Miss Mary Dixon...1910 - 1925
Miss E.J. Keates...1925 - 1930
Miss Nora W, Moore ....1930 - 1947

Senior children move to Linacre Lane site in 1947 and amalgamate with Gray Street children.

ORRELL JUNIOR BOYS' DEPARTMENT
Mr. G. C. O. Hall ....1947 - 1964

ORRELL JUNIOR GIRLS' DEPARTMENT
Miss Nora Moore ....1947 - 1952
Miss E. M. White ....1952 - 1964

ORRELL INFANTS' DEPARTMENT
Miss Margaret E. Swift......................................1910 - 1926
Miss Rose E. Owen ....1926 - 1950
Miss E.E. Denson .... 1950 - 1953
Miss S.C. Robertson ....1953 - 1960
Miss P.I. Williams ....1960 - 1971
Mrs. Shirley Townsend ....1971 - 1974
Miss Margaret Smith (acting) ....1974 - 1975

In 1964 Junior Girls' and Boys' departments amalgamate.

ORRELL JUNIOR MIXED DEPARTMENT
Mr. Bryan T. Scott ....1964 - 1974
Mr. Ted Williams (acting) ....1974 - 1975

The Junior and Infant departments amalgamate in 1975

ORRELL J.M.I. SCHOOL
Mr. David Cheetham..1975 - 1987
Mr. Robert J. Branch..1987 - 1998
Ms. Jan Smoult ....1998 - 2006

School closes 2006 and amalgamates with Roberts C.P. to form SPRINGWELL PARK C.P. SCHOOL with Ms J. Smoult as Headteacher.

■ OUR LADY OF WALSINGHAM ROMAN CATHOLIC SCHOOL 1960

OUR LADY OF WALSINGHAM INFANT DEPARTMENT
Miss F. Mahon ....1960 -
Miss V. Dempsey ....196 - 1991
Mrs. Stella M. Smith..1991 - 2006

OUR LADY OF WALSINGHAM J. M. DEPARTMENT

Mr. Bernard Dwyer ....1960 - 1971
Mr. Reg Baden ....1971 - 1986
Mr. M. J. Halford ....1987 - 2006

The Infant and Junior departments to amalgamate in 2006

■ PRINCESS ROYAL J.M.I. SCHOOL
Miss A.D. Mills..1956 - 1967
Mr. O.E. Hughes ....1967 -
Mr. Proctor .... -
Miss Val Rowntree.. - 1987
Mrs. Gillian Jones ....1987 - 1990

■ ROBERTS COUNCIL SCHOOL

ROBERTS TEMPORARY PRIMARY SCHOOL 1927
Miss Emily Pritchard ....1927 - 1931

ROBERTS SENIOR BOYS' DEPARTMENT
Mr. E.J. Pengelly...1931 - 1936
Mr. A. M. Fletcher ....1936 - 1942
Mr. G. C. O. Hall (acting)................................1942 - 1945
Mr. A.M. Fletcher ....1945 - 1954

Senior boys move to St. George of England Secondary Modern School in 1954.

ROBERTS SENIOR GIRLS' DEPARTMENT
Miss Mabelle Bond...1931 - 1946
Miss S.H. Morley...1947 - 1962
Miss Olwyn Adams...1962 - 1968

Senior Girls move to St. George of England Mixed Secondary School in 1968.

ROBERTS JUNIOR AND INFANT DEPARTMENT
Mrs. Eleanor Kay...1931 - 1935

Miss Elizabeth Jones..............................1935 - 1954

The Infant and Junior children are divided into separate departments in 1954.

ROBERTS INFANT DEPARTMENT
Miss Jeanie Stewart ....1954 - 1975
Miss Margaret Smith ....1975 - 1981

ROBERTS JUNIOR DEPARTMENT
Mrs. E.M. White ....1964 - 1968
Mr. David Mawhinney.......................1968 - 1981

The Infant and Junior departments amalgamate in 1981

ROBERTS J.M.I. SCHOOL
Miss Margaret Smith ....1981 - 1991
Mr. Kenneth Bold ....1991 - 1993
Mrs. Tracey Moore ....1993 - 1999
Mrs. Marion. Ainslie..........................1999 - 2003
Mrs. Sarah Howard ....2003 - 2005
Mrs. Kay Ramsay ....2005 - 2006

School closes 2006 and amalgamates with Orrell C.P. School to form SPRINGWELL PARK C.P. SCHOOL

■ **ST. GEORGE OF ENGLAND BOYS' SECONDARY MODERN SCHOOL**
Mr. Alec Fletcher ....1954 - 1968

ST. GEORGE OF ENGLAND MIXED SEC. MOD. SCHOOL
Miss Olwyn Adams..............................1968 - 1972

ST. GEORGE OF ENGLAND COMPREHENSIVE SCHOOL
Mr. Terry Broughton ....1972 - 1974
Mr. John Evans ....1974 - 1990

Mr. Ralph Davies (acting) ....1988 - 1989
Mr. Bob Madgin (acting) ....1989 - 1990
Mr. Vernon J. Schwarz........................1990 - 2006
Mrs. Lynne Wise ....2006 -

■ **SALISBURY ROAD BOARD SCHOOL 1885, COUNCIL 1903**

SALISBURY ROAD SENIOR BOYS' DEPARTMENT
Mr. James Vernon Brown ....1885 - 1892
Mr. J. J. H. Stringer (acting) ....1892 - 1892
Mr. James Blair ....1892 - 1895
Mr. Stanley Leigh (died 1926).............1895 - 1924
Mr. E. J. Pengelly...............................1924 - 1927

SALISBURY ROAD SENIOR GIRLS' DEPARTMENT
Miss A. E. Brack ....1885 - 1890
Miss Eleanor McKenzie ....1890 - 1894
Miss Alice Leipnitz..............................1894 - 1897
Miss M.E. Ramsey...............................1897 - 1900
Miss Elizabeth Chadwick ....1900 - 1927

The Senior Boys and Girls move to Gray Street in 1927

SALISBURY ROAD JUNIOR BOYS' DEPARTMENT
Miss Cordelia Corbett..........................1885 - 1893
Miss Mary E. Dixon ....1893 - 1910
Miss A. E. Shepherd ....1910 - 1925
Mr. John Dixon ....1927 - 1942

SALISBURY ROAD JUNIOR GIRLS' DEPARTMENT
Miss A.J. Mathias ....1885 - 1892
Miss Sarah Addis ....1892 - 1895
Miss Isabella Underwood ....1895 - 1900
Miss C. E. Tanner ....1900 - 1925
Miss A. E. Shepherd ....1925 - 1931
Miss E.M. Boardman ....1931 - 1942

SALISBURY ROAD INFANT DEPARTMENT
Miss H. Wharham ....1885 - 1924
Miss E. J. Morgan ....1924 - 1942

SALISBURY ROAD JMI SCHOOL
Miss E. M. Boardman..........................1942 - 1954

1954 Junior children transfer to Gray Street School and Gray Street Infants transfer to Salisbury Road.

SALISBURY ROAD INFANT SCHOOL
Miss E. M. Boardman..........................1954 - 1960
Mrs. I. Spence ....1960 - 1972

Salisbury Road Infants and Gray Street Junior Schools close in 1972. A new school, THOMAS GRAY, opens near to the old Salisbury Road School site.

THOMAS GRAY INFANTS' SCHOOL
Mrs. J. L. Seddon ....1972 - 1983
Miss Elizabeth Kent............................1983 - 1989
Mrs. Margaret Lawrence nee Kelly .....1989 - 1990
Mrs. Eileen Walsh...............................1990 - 2004

THOMAS GRAY JUNIOR SCHOOL
Mr. John Horn ....1972 - 1983
Mr. R. Gareth Potter ....1983 - 2004

THOMAS GRAY J.M.I. SCHOOL from 2004
Mr. R. Gareth Potter...........................2004 -

■ **ST. ALEXANDER'S ROMAN CATHOLIC SCHOOL.**

ST. ALEXANDER'S BOYS' DEPARTMENT
Mr. Thomas Wood ....1879 - 1906
Mr. J. Bradshaw ....1906 - 1915

ST. ALEXANDER'S GIRLS' DEPARTMENT
Sisters of Notre Dame......................................1879 - 1915

ST. ALEXANDER'S INFANTS' DEPARTMENT
Sisters of Notre Dame......................................1879 - 1915

■ ST. BENETS ROMAN CATHOLIC SCHOOL, LANCASHIRE
Miss K. Catterall .... -
Miss Lynch .... - 1958

Netherton Village JMI School taken over by Bootle from Lancashire in 1958.

ST. BENET'S JMI SCHOOL
Miss M. J. Doyle ....1958 - 1963

Following an increase in pupil numbers, school is divided into separate Infant and Junior departments in 1963.

ST. BENET'S INFANT DEPARTMENT
Miss M. J. Doyle......................................1963 - 1981

ST. BENET'S JUNIOR MIXED DEPARTMENT
Mr. Bernard Gregg..................................1963 - 1981

ST. BENET'S J.M.I. SCHOOL from 1981
Mr. Bernard Gregg..................................1981 - 1985
Mr. Christopher Byrne ....1985 - 2005

ST. BENEDICT'S PRIMARY SCHOOL 2005
Amalgamation of St Benet's & St. Raymond's Schools.
Mr. Chris Vaudrey....................................2005 -

■ ST. THOMAS AQUINAS ROMAN CATHOLIC MIXED SECONDARY SCHOOL 1961
Senior boys from Netherton Schools plus some from St. James' and St. Joan's.
Mr. P. Hagan (Boys) ....1961 - 1965
Miss N. O'Malley (Sister Rosario) (Girls) ....1963 - 1965

In 1965 St. Thomas Aquinas School becomes a Boys' Secondary Modern School.

ST. THOMAS AQUINAS BOYS' SECONDARY MODERN SCHOOL 1965
Mr. P. Hagan ....1965 - 1981

Until their school is opened the girls use part of St. Thomas Aquinas' School and also huts on the old Linacre Fever Hospital site in Linacre Lane.

ST. CATHERINE'S GIRLS' SECONDARY SCHOOL
Mrs. J. Doyle (acting head Jan-Apr.)..................1965 - 1965
Miss M. E. Breen (Mother Regina)....................1965 - 1981

In 1981 St. Catherine's School is renamed St. Ambrose Barlow R.C. High School. St Thomas Aquinas Boys' School is closed; pupils move to St. Ambrose Barlow creating a co-educational High School.

ST. AMBROSE BARLOW HIGH SCHOOL 1981
Mr. Victor McClelland ....1981 - 1997
Mr. A. V. Traynor....................................1997 - 2005
Mr. Paul Davidson ....2005 -

■ ST. JAMES' ROMAN CATHOLIC SCHOOL founded 1846
Miss Kathy Coffey....................................1846 - 1879
Sisters of the Sacred Heart of Mary ....1879 - 1900

ST. JAMES' SENIOR BOYS' DEPARTMENT
Mr. Jonathan Smith ....1900 - 1923
Mr. J. Clinton ....1923 - 1934
Mr. J. O'Connor ....1934 - 1940
Mr. P. Kearney ....1940 - 1961

St. James' Boys amalgamate with St. Joan of Arc's Boys in 1961 on St Joan's site. Mr. P. Kearney becomes deputy of the combined school until his retirement in 1964. Some pupils move to St. Thomas Aquinas School in Netherton

ST. JAMES' SENIOR GIRLS' DEPARTMENT
Miss Coogan ....1900 - 1909
Miss T. Crean ....1909 - 1921
Miss M.F. Delamere (Sister St. Joseph) ....1922 - 1946
Miss H. M. Browne (Sister Bernadine)..............1947 - 1985

St. Joan's senior girls move to St. James' school site in 1961. Senior girls from St. Winefride's join them in 1964. The school closes in 1985; pupils transfer to Savio Co-Educational High School.

ST. JAMES' JUNIOR AND INFANT DEPARTMENT
Miss I. Whelan......................................1900 - 1906

Juniors and Infants become separate departments in 1906

ST. JAMES' JUNIOR MIXED DEPARTMENT
Mrs. M.B. Reid......................................1906 - 1917

Junior girls and boys become separate departments, 1917

ST. JAMES' JUNIOR BOYS' DEPARTMENT
Mrs M. B. Reid......................................1917 - 1939
Miss E. Fitzgerald ....1939 - 1947
Miss H. O'Dea (Sister Cuthbert) ....1947 - 1962

ST. JAMES' JUNIOR GIRLS' DEPARTMENT
Miss B. M. Brennan..................................1917 - 1924

Miss Glenn (Sister St. Joseph)..........................1924 - 1954
Miss B. Gormally (Sister Ignatius)....................1954 - 1962

ST. JAMES' JUNIOR MIXED DEPARTMENT 1962
Miss B. Gormally (Sister Ignatius)....................1962 - 1971
Mr. Stephen Pope ....1971 - 1980

ST. JAMES' INFANT DEPARTMENT
Miss I. Whelan...1906 - 1910
Miss E. Beesley ....1910 - 1939
Sister Honora Coleman....................................1939 - 1956
Sister Helena ....1956 - 1968
Sister Christina ....1968 - 1980

The Infant and Junior departments amalgamate in 1980

ST. JAMES' PRIMARY SCHOOL
Mr. John Rourke ....1980 - 1996
Mr. David Ryan..1996 - 2000
Mr. Mark Rigby ....2000 - 2006

St. James' and St. Joan's R.C. Primary Schools will amalgamate on the St. James's site in 2007 and the school will be renamed.

■ ST. JAMES SELECT ROMAN CATHOLIC HIGHER GRADE SCHOOL 1891

BOYS' DEPARTMENT
Mr. J.T. Hogan ....1891 - 1915
Mr. A.H. Roberts (died in post) ....1915 - 1926
Mr. W. Heyes ....1926 - 1939

GIRLS' DEPARTMENT
Sisters Sacred Heart of Mary...........................1891 - 1925
Miss M. McCall ....1905 - 1907
Miss E. Beesley ....1907 - 1910

Miss J. W. Reagan (acting) ....1910 - 1910
Miss D. Honan ....1925 - 1933
Miss N. O'Dea ....1933 - 1936
Miss E. Fitzgerald ....1936 - 1939

INFANT DEPARTMENT
Miss T. Crean ....1891 - 1907
Sisters Sacred Heart of Mary...........................1907 - 1939

■ ST. JOAN OF ARC ROMAN CATHOLIC SCHOOLS 1935

ST. JOAN OF ARC JUNIOR MIXED DEPARTMENT
Miss Catherine Rafferty...................................1935 - 1960
Sister Lucy ....1960 - 1966
Mr. Joseph E. Jones ....1966 - 1980

ST. JOAN OF ARC INFANT DEPARTMENT
Miss E. Wilcox ....1935 - 1945
Miss M.E. Finen ....1945 - 1959
Miss Molly Draper..1959 - 1980

The Infant and Junior departments amalgamate in 1980

ST. JOAN OF ARC J.M.I. SCHOOL
Sister Bridget Purcell ....1980 - 1990
Mr. Stephen J. Sanderson ....1990 - 2006

St. Joan's JMI amalgamate with St. James' JMI on the St. James' site in 2006.

ST. JOAN'S MIXED SECONDARY SCHOOL
Mr. Stephen J. Brown ....1951 - 1972

In 1961 some of the senior boys from St. James' move to St. Joan's School while others go to the newly opened St. Thomas Aquinas School in Netherton. The school closes in 1972 and the pupils transfer to the Salesian High School.

■ ST. JOHN'S CHURCH of ENGLAND NATIONAL SCHOOL 1879

ST JOHN'S BOYS' DEPARTMENT 1829 -1938
Mr. Adam Kay..1879 - 1911
Mr. Laurence D. Wood.....................................1911 - 1925
Mr. J. T. Hall ....1925 - 1930

ST JOHN'S GIRLS' DEPARTMENT 1879 - 1929
Miss Isabella Ferryman....................................1879 - 1901
Miss Rae ....1901 - 1909
Miss McCarthy ....1909 - 1926
Miss E. H. Gill ....1926 - 1929

ST JOHN'S INFANT DEPARTMENT 1879 - 1929
Miss Agnes Parry ....1879 - 1901
Miss E. E. Appleton ....1901 - 1923
Miss L. Roden ....1923 - 1929

ST JOHN'S GIRLS' AND INFANTS' DEPARTMENT from 1929 - 1930
Miss L. Roden ....1929 - 1930

In 1930 following the reorganisation of the Church of England Schools in the Borough the senior girls go to Christ Church and the senior boys to St. Mary's. From this point St. John's caters for children aged 5-10.

ST. JOHN'S JUNIOR GIRLS' AND INFANT DEPARTMENT
Miss F. Tickle..1930 - 1938

ST. JOHN'S JUNIOR BOYS' DEPARTMENT
Mr. J. T. Hall ....1930 - 1938

In 1938 the Junior Boys' department amalgamates with the Junior Girls' and Infant department to form a J.M.I. School.

ST JOHN'S J.M.I. SCHOOL 1938 - 1949
Mr. R. Murray ....1938 - 1949

In 1949 the school becomes a County Primary School.

ST. JOHN'S COUNTY PRIMARY SCHOOL 1949 - 1967
Mr. R. Murray ....1949 - 1951
Miss M. Weeks ....1951 - 1964
Mrs. E. Miller ....1965 - 1967

■ ST. JOSEPH'S ROMAN CATHOLIC CENTRAL SCHOOL 1926-1932
Brother J. I. O'Leary (Xavier Brothers) ....1926 - 1932

ST. MARTIN'S SECONDARY SCHOOL FOR BOYS 1932-1964
School run by the Xavier Brothers. ....1932 - 1964

SALESIAN GRAMMAR SCHOOL FOR BOYS 1964
School run by the Salesian Brothers.
Rev. Fr. A. Keogh S.D.B. ....1964 - 1971

Selection ends 1971/2; school becomes comprehensive.

SALESIAN HIGH SCHOOL FOR BOYS
Rev. Fr. Maurice Gordon S.D.B. ....1971 - 1985

In 1985 Salesian High School becomes co-educational.

SAVIO CO-EDUCATIONAL HIGH SCHOOL 1985
Rev. Anthony Bailey S.D.B. ....1985 - 1995
Rev. J. L. Mageean S.D.B...............................1995 - 2005
Rev J. Briody S.D.B. ....2005 -

ST. AUGUSTINES MIXED SECONDARY MODERN SCHOOL 1963-71
Mr. G.F. O'Donnell (died in post) ....1963 - 1969

Mr. J.V. Doyle (acting) ....1969 - 1971

In 1971 the senior boys move to the Salesian High School. St Augustine's becomes a high school for girls.

ST. AUGUSTINE'S GIRLS' HIGH SCHOOL 1971-1985
Miss Joan Williams...1971 - 1979
Mrs Ann Howard ....1979 - 1985

■ ST. MARY'S CHURCH OF ENGLAND NATIONAL SCHOOL

ST. MARY'S BOYS & GIRLS ALL AGE SCHOOL
Mr. H. Roberts ....1835 - 1852
Mr. R.J. Bentley ....1852 - 1861
Mr. E.W.R. Pearson ....1861 - 1865

ST. MARY'S GIRLS' DEPARTMENT (ALL AGE)
Miss S. Tilling..1861 - 1864
Miss Sansbury ....1864 - 1865
Miss Marsh ....1865 - 1866
Miss J. Parr ....1866 - 1870
Miss Alice Wilson..1870 - 1876
Mrs. M.A. Smith ....1876 - 1885
Mrs. Scott..1885 - 1914
Mrs. H.F. Bargery ....1914 - 1926
Miss B.M. Smith ....1926 - 1930

In 1930 the Senior Girls from St. Mary's and St. John's Schools transfer to Christ Church School.

ST. MARY'S BOYS' DEPARTMENT (ALL AGE)
Mr. W. Callister..1865 - 1872
Mr. James Gill..1872 - 1910
Mr. W.W. Warburton ....1910 - 1931
Mr. McKelvie Stewart ....1931 - 1938

In 1930 the Senior Boys from Christ Church and St. John's School move to St. Mary's. In 1938 the Senior Boys move to Balliol Secondary School and St. Mary's becomes a Primary School.

ST. MARY'S JUNIOR BOYS' DEPARTMENT
Mr. J.R.D. Jones...1938 - 1945

ST. MARY'S JUNIOR GIRLS' DEPARTMENT
Miss B.M. Smith..1930 - 1945

In 1945 Junior Girls' and Boys' departments amalgamate.

ST. MARY'S JUNIOR MIXED DEPARTMENT
Mr. J.R.D. Jones...1945 - 1956
Mr. William Rigby ....1956 - 1968

ST. MARY'S INFANT DEPARTMENT
Miss Mary Bibby ....1856 - 1893
Miss A. L. Grosvenor ....1893 - 1929
Mrs. E. Steinley ....1929 - 1961
Miss M. Bowen...1961 - 1968

The School becomes a Junior and Infant School in 1968

ST. MARY'S J. M. I. SCHOOL
Mr. William Rigby ....1968 - 1972
Mr. Colin Sands (acting Jan-July) ....1972 - 1972
Mr. William Rigby ....1972 - 1973
Mr. Tom Wilkinson ....1973 - 1990
Mr. Tom M. Brooksbank ....1990 - 1996
Miss Christine Richards...................................1996 - 2003
Mrs. Christine Thursfield..................................2003 - 2005

■ ST. MONICA'S ROMAN CATHOLIC SCHOOL (Fernhill Rd site)
Miss B. Holoan (Sister Agatha).........................1926 - 1937

1937 the school divides into two departments: Boys and Girls / Infants.

ST. MONICA'S GIRLS' & INFANT DEPARTMENT (Fernhill Rd site)

Miss B. Holoan (Sister Agatha)..........................1937 - 1947

ST. MONICA'S BOYS' DEPARTMENT (Aintree Rd site)

Mr. W. Heyes ....1937 - 1947

1947 the senior pupils become a separate department. The remaining pupils become Junior Boys and Junior Girls / Infants.

ST. MONICA'S MIXED SENIOR DEPARTMENT (Linacre Hospital site)

Mr. G. F. O'Donnell ....1947 - 1964

1964 Senior boys and girls move to the newly opened St. Augustine's Mixed Secondary School in King Avenue

ST. MONICA'S JUNIOR GIRLS' AND INFANT DEPARTMENT (Fernhill Rd site)

Miss B. Holoan (Sister Agatha)..........................1947 - 1949

In 1949 the Junior Girls and Infants become separate departments.

ST. MONICA'S JUNIOR GIRLS' DEPARTMENT (Fernhill Rd site)

Miss Grant (Sister Margaret May).....................1949 - 1968

ST. MONICA'S JUNIOR BOYS' DEPARTMENT (Aintree Rd site)

Mr. W. Heyes ....1947 - 1950
Mr. W. Redmond..1951 - 1960
Mr. P. T. McSweeney ....1960 - 1968

ST. MONICA'S INFANT DEPARTMENT (Fernhill Rd site)

Miss S. M. Brennan ....1949 - 1951
Sister Carmella...1951 - 1960
Sister Christopher ....1960 - 1971
Miss Sheila Cheyne ....1971 - 1989

In 1968 the Junior Boys and Girls departments amalgamate on the Aintree Rd site. Some Junior Girls remain on the Fernhill Rd site, the last ones moving to the Aintree Rd site in 1973.

ST. MONICA'S JUNIOR MIXED DEPARTMENT (Mostly Aintree Rd site)

P.T. McSweeney...1968 - 1970
Mr. A.F. Hughes ....1970 - 1981
Mr. Brian M. Mullroy ....1981 - 1989

The Infant department is closed in 1989 and the Infants join the Juniors on the Aintree Rd site.

ST. MONICA'S J.M.I. SCHOOL (Aintree Rd site)

Mr. Brian M. Mullroy ....1989 - 2002
Mr. Andrew Windsor ....2002 - 2004
Mr. Paul Kinsella ....2004 -

■ ST. OSWALD'S CHURCH of ENGLAND JUNIOR SCHOOL 1959

Mr. Godfrey Doubleday ....1959 - 1970
Mr. Eric Rowley...1970 - 1974

ST. OSWALD'S COUNTY INFANT SCHOOL

Miss Barbara Edwards ....1960 - 1974

ST. OSWALD'S J.M.I. SCHOOL

Mr. Eric Rowley...1974 - 1978
Mr. David Walker (acting) ....1978 - 1980

Mr. Alan Goodall ....1980 - 1996
Mrs. Margaret F. Ellams ....1996 -

■ ST. PAUL'S SPECIAL SCHOOL 1957 later ROWAN PARK

Mr. G. E. Newns ....1957 - 1980
Mrs. A. Oldhams.. -

■ ST. RAYMOND'S ROMAN CATHOLIC J.M.I. SCHOOL 1968

Mr. Harry McGee..1968 - 1981
Mr. Joseph McKeating (acting) ....1981 - 1982
Mr. Stephen McKenna ....1982 - 1991
Mr. Christopher T. Vaudrey ....1991 - 2005

St. Raymond's and St. Benet's schools amalgamate on the St. Benet's site with Mr. Christopher Vaudrey as Headteacher

■ ST. ROBERT BELLARMINES ROMAN CATHOLIC J.M.I. SCHOOL 1935

Mr. D. Kirby ....1935 - 1961
Mr. Michael Lyonette ....1961 - 1985
Miss Eileen M. McManus ....1985 - 1997
Miss Anne Titherington ....1997 -

■ ST. WINEFRIDE'S ROMAN CATHOLIC SCHOOL 1903

ST. WINEFRIDE'S BOYS' DEPARTMENT

Mr. P. O'Brian...1903 - 1930
Mr. J. Toolan ....1930 - 1955
Mr. T.Nevin (died in post) ....1955 - 1964
Mr. G. F. Rogan ....1964 - 1967

ST. WINEFRIDE'S GIRLS' DEPARTMENT

Mrs. Kearney ....1903 - 1924
Miss Mary White ....1925 - 1930

Miss E. M. Neville (acting) ....1930 - 1931
Miss E. Shaw ....1931 - 1951
Sister Therese ....1952 - 1967
Sister Hilary ....1967 - 1971

In 1952 The Girls' department divides into Junior and Senior Girls. The Senior Girls move to the St. Martin's College building in Stanley Road and the Junior Girls to a new building in Pembroke Road.

St. Winefride's Senior Girls amalgamate with St. James at St. Joan's senior girls on the St. James campus.

ST. WINEFRIDE'S JUNIOR GIRLS
Sister Kieran ....1952 - 1968
Sister Marie Patrice..1968 - 1982

ST. WINEFRIDE'S JUNIOR BOYS
Mr. James Fearon...1954 - 1963
Mr. R.P. Moss..1963 - 1967
Mr. Joseph Murdoch ....1967 - 1982

The Junior Girls and Boys amalgamate in 1982

ST. WINEFRIDE'S AND ST. RICHARD'S J.M. from 1990
Mr. Andrew Windsor ....1982 - 1990
Mr. John W. Dolan..1990 - 1999

INFANTS
Miss Noble ....1903 - 1909
Miss O'Shea..1909 - 1915
Miss M. Vincent...1915 - 1923
Miss Elizabeth Shea ....1923 - 1927
Miss E. Shaw ....1927 - 1951
Miss G.L. Moore...1951 - 1961
Miss M. Jones ....1961 - 1970
Miss Kathleen Cunningham ....1970 - 1991

Mrs. Veronica Houlton......................................1991 - 1999

Infant and Junior departments amalgamate in 1999

ST. WINEFRIDE'S AND ST. RICHARD'S J.M.I from 1999
Mr. John W. Dolan ....1999 - 2005

■ STERRIX C. P. SCHOOL 1955 -1976 DALEACRE from 1976
Mrs. A.H. Jones ....1955 - 1967
Miss A.D. Mills..1967 - 1974
Mr. Colin Sands ....1974 - 1980
Mr. David Williams ....1980 - 1985
Mrs. Margaret Cooke ....1985 - 1986
Mrs. Dorice Davidson (acting) ....1986 - 1988
Mrs Pat Grice ....1988 - 1991
Mrs Margaret Carrington ....1991 - 1995
Mr. Eric Morris ....1995 - 1998
Mr. Colin Coleman ....1998 - 2002
Mrs. V. Adams ....2003 - 2004
Mrs. Judith Aspinwall ....2003 - 2005

■ THE GRANGE J.M.I. SCHOOL 1968-1969
Mr. Harold Pryce ....1968 - 1969

THE GRANGE JUNIOR SCHOOL 1969-1981
Mr. Harold Pryce ....1969 - 1981

THE GRANGE INFANT SCHOOL 1969-1981
Miss Catherine L. McLauchlin ....1969 - 1981

1981 amalgamation of Infant and Junior departments.

THE GRANGE J.M.I. SCHOOL
Mr. Harold Pryce ....1981 - 1983
Mr. Brian Norbury ....1983 -

■ MERTON SCHOOL (4 Merton Road)
Mr. Reginald Tollitt 1927

BOOTLE CHURCHES AND CLERGY

■ ANGLICAN DIOCESE of CHESTER (1880) LIVERPOOL
Bishop Charles James Blomfield (Chester)........1820 - 1828
Bishop John Bird Sumner (Chester)..................1828 - 1848
Bishop John Graham (Chester)..........................1848 - 1865
Bishop William Jackson (Chester) ....1865 - 1880
Bishop Charles Ryle (Liverpool)...................... 1880 - 1900
Bishop Dr. Francis James Chavasse (Liverpool) ..1900 - 1923
Bishop Albert Augustus David (Liverpool)........1923 - 1944
Bishop Clifford Arthur Martin (Liverpool) ....1944 - 1965
Bishop Stuart Yanworth Blanche (Liverpool) ....1966 - 1975
Bishop Dr. David Stuart Sheppard (Liverpool)..1975 - 1999
Bishop James Jones (Liverpool) ....1999 -

● CHURCH OF ENGLAND CHURCHES
Persons named served as Vicars unless otherwise stated.

CHRIST CHURCH BOOTLE
Rev. Edward Lushington Mather......................1866 - 1879
Rev. Terry Avison Scott ....1879 - 1887
Rev. Francis Charles Masters ....1887 - 1893
Rev. A. Wynne Williams ....1893 - 1917
Rev. Walter S. Mather ....1917 - 1921
Rev. Edward Mayson ....1921 - 1945
Rev. William Chipping ....1945 - 1961
Rev. Robert E. Dennis ....1961 - 1975
Rev. Ralph Werrell.......................................1975 - 1980
Rev. Rob Millington ....1980 - 1989
Rev. David Johnston (Priest in Charge) ....1989 - 1991
Rev. Tom Rich (Priest in Charge)....................1992 - 1993
Rev. Tom Rich ....1993 -

ST. ANDREW'S LITHERLAND

Rev. George Jackson	1903 - 1925
Rev. Daniel Edward Hughes	1925 - 1932
Rev. Henry George Wheeler	1932 - 1936
Rev. Richard Albert Rostron	1936 - 1947
Rev. Bertram Philip Knight	1947 - 1956
Rev. Thomas Fisher Robinson	1956 - 1962
Rev. Fred Harrison	1962 - 1975
Rev. Barry Walter John Lomax (P.I.C.)	1976 - 1978
(also Vicar of St. Matthew's 1973 - 78)	
Rev. Richard Stephens (P.I.C.)	1979 - 1983
(also Vicar of St. Matthew's 1979 - 1989)	
Rev. James Miller P.I.C.	1983 - 1985
Rev. James Miller	1985 - 1989
Rev. Clive Henry Kirke (P. I. C.)	1989 - 1998
Rev. Roger John Driver (P.I.C.)	1998 -

ST. JOHN'S BOOTLE

Rev. Richard Wareing Bardsley	1864 - 1883
Rev. Charles Lester	1883 - 1918
Rev. William Lloyd Musgrave Protheroe	1918 - 1925
Rev. Samuel Herbert Breeze	1925 - 1941
Joint benefice with Christ Church Bootle	
Rev. William Hamilton Herring	1957 - 1958

ST. JOHN AND ST. JAMES BOOTLE

Rev Colin Dawson Curate in Charge)	1900 - 1911
Rev Colin Dawson	1911 - 1917
Rev. Edward Wallbanke-Jones	1917 - 1935
Rev. George Mackereth Mawdsley	1935 - 1943
Rev. Francis Clement Musgrave-Brown	1943 - 1954
Rev. Eric Russell	1954 - 1957
Rev. Arthur Ernest Charman	1957 - 1973
Rev. David Vaughan Rouch	1974 - 1996
Rev. Richard James Graham Panter	1996 -

ST. LEONARD'S BOOTLE

Rev. James Denton Thompson	1889 - 1894
Rev. Rev. Edward John Steintz	1894 - 1905
Rev. Ernest Augustus Chard	1905 - 1911
Rev. John Campbell Gray Mercer	1911 - 1924
Rev. William Herbert Lewis	1925 - 1935
Rev. John James Armitage	1935 - 1943
Rev. Arthur Stanley Adamson	1943 - 1957
Rev. John Fredrick Mockford	1957 - 1964
Rev. Philip Gasgoine	1965 - 1971
Rev. Brian Cave	1971 - 1975
Rev. Elliot Malcomb Duthie (P. I. C.)	1976 - 1978
Rev. Elliot Malcomb Duthie	1978 - 1981
Rev. Charles David Benge	1982 - 2002
Rev Roger John Driver	2002 -

ST. MARY'S BOOTLE

Rev. John Gladstone	1827 - 1846
Rev. J. Crump	1846 - 1879
Rev. Edward Francis Neep	1879 - 1889
Rev. John Bullen	1889 - 1913
Rev. George Atkinson	1913 - 1922
Rev. Percy Denil Maddock	1922 - 1928
Rev. Frederick William Lloyd	1928 - 1948
Rev. Arthur John Ostley	1948 - 1951
Rev. Deryck Barnard Garland	1951 - 1957
Rev. William Hamilton Herring	1958 - 1961
(Vicar of St Mary with St. John)	
Interregnum	1961 - 1963
Rev. Joseph Kitts (Curate in Charge)	1963 - 1966
Rev. Reginald Wilfred Burrows (C. I. C.)	1966 - 1969
Rev Geoffrey Gifford Howarth (C. I. C.)	1969 - 1971
Rev Brian Cave Vicar of St Leonard's	1971 - 1975
Interregnum	1975 - 1977

ST. MARY'S with ST.PAUL'S

Rev. Peter William Plunkett	1977 - 1981

Rev. Andrew Hetherington	1982 - 1993
Rev. Peter Harry Jordan	1994 - 2002
Interregnum	2002 - 2005

ST. MATTHEW'S BOOTLE

Rev. Arthur West Oliver	1887 - 1902
Rev. W. Harry Robert	1903 - 1918
Rev. Clement A. McCormick	1918 - 1930
Rev. William L. St. John	1930 - 1936
Rev. Cyril Henry Winstanley	1936 - 1941
Rev. L.A. Thomas	1941 - 1943
Rev. Ernest Lyons Penley	1943 - 1950
Rev. James William Roxburgh	1950 - 1956
Rev. John Gaunt Hunter	1956 - 1962
Rev. Denis William Gatenby	1963 - 1972
Rev. Barry Walter John Lomax	1972 - 1978
Rev. Richard Stephens	1979 - 1989
Rev. Christopher Jones	1989 - 1999
Rev. Roger John Driver	1999 -

ST. OSWALD'S NETHERTON

Rev. Paul Edward Turton	1957 - 1964
Rev. George Orman Farran	1964 - 1973
Also Rector of Sefton	1969 - 1973
Rev. Robert Anthony Wilkes	1977 - 1981
Rev. Richard Mark Spurin	1982 - 1985
Rev. Alistair Alexander Ross	1987 - 1994
Rev. Andrew James Edwards	1995 - 2002
Rev. Nicholas Anthony Wells	2003 -

■ ROMAN CATHOLIC ARCHDIOCESE of LIVERPOOL

Bishop George Brown	1850 - 1856
Bishop Alexander Goss	1856 - 1872
Bishop Bernard O'Reilly	1873 - 1894
Bishop Thomas Whiteside	1894 - 1911
Archbishop Thomas Whiteside	1911 - 1921
Archbishop Frederick William Keating	1921 - 1928

Archbishop Richard Downey ....1928 - 1953
Archbishop William Godfrey ....1953 - 1957
Archbishop John Carmel Heenan ....1957 - 1964
Archbishop George Andrew Beck ....1964 - 1976
Archbishop Derek Warlock................................1976 - 1996
Archbishop Patrick Altham Kelly.....................1996 -

● ROMAN CATHOLIC CHURCHES

Persons named served as parish priests unless otherwise stated.

HOLY SEPULCHRE CHURCH AND CONVENT FORD
Rev. J. Aylward ....1880 - 1895
Rev. Thomas Brown ....1885 - 1895
Rev. Charles Reynolds............................1895 - 1901
Rev. Patrick Monaghan............................1901 - 1910
Rev. James Lowry....................................1910 - 1925
Rev. William Joseph Daly........................1925 - 1931
Rev. Joseph Ignatius Dickinson ....1931 - 1937
Parish of English Martyrs Litherland ....1937 - 1954
Rev Gerrard W. Walker (Holy Ghost Parish ......1954 -

HOLY GHOST later HOLY SPIRIT founded 1953
Rev. Gerrard W. Walker ....1954 - 1959
Rev Michael O'Donoghue ....1959 - 1978
Rev Donald Coffey ....1978 - 1986
Rev. Terence Dooley ....1986 - 1991
Rev. John Harris.....................................1991 -

OUR LADY OF WALSINGHAM (founded 1956)
Rev Robert Slattery.................................1960 - 1971
Rev. John Pennington ....1971 - 1979
Rev Geoffrey Leo Lynch ....1979 - 1986
Rev. Brian Crane.....................................1986 - 1987
Rev Peter Fox ....1987 - 1991
Rev. Anthony Eagleton ....1996 -

ST. ALEXANDER'S (founded 1862 closed 1991)
Rev. Edward Powell................................1866 - 1885
Rev. Michael Beggan, later Canon ....1885 - 1910
Rev. Joseph Keagan ....1910 - 1923
Rev. Bernard A. Kavanagh ....1923 - 1929
Rev. Canon Joseph H. Kelly ....1929 - 1950
Rev Michael Nugent ....1951 - 1960
Parish amalgamates with St. Richards.

ST. RICHARD'S (founded 1938)
Rev. Canon Joseph H. Kelly ....1938 - 1950
Rev Louis Coupe ....1951 - 1952
Rev Charles Taylor ....1952 - 1960

ST. ALEXANDER'S with ST. RICHARDS
Rev. Michael Nugent ....1960 - 1968
Rev. Pat Ryan ....1968 - 1985
Rev. Pat McCambridge ....1985 - 1991
Rev, Bernard Parker ....1991 - 1998
Rev. Michael O'Meara ....1998 - 2005
St Monica's takes over responsibility for the parish
Rev. Pat Sexton ....2005 -

ST. BENET'S NETHERTON founded 1697
Rev. Thomas M. Shepherd.......................1870 - 1887
Rev. John O. Burchall ....1887 - 1891
Rev. Henry Wulsten Perkins ....1891 - 1911
Rev O. P. O'Hear ....1911 - 1913
Rev Benedict. Placid Griffin....................1913 - 1925
Rev Augustus Gregory Green ....1925 - 1936
Rev. R. Vincent Gilbertson ....1936 - 1946
Rev. Richard Osmund Campbell ....1946 - 1958
Rev. Francis J. Danher ....1958 - 1959
Rev. Samuel Park ....1959 - 1960
Rev. Thomas Turner ....1960 - 1968
Rev, Vincent O'Reilly..............................1968 - 1993
Rev Joseph Feeley ....1993 - 2003

ST. JAMES (founded 1845)
Rev. Henry Sharples ....1845 - 1846
Rev. George Fisher ....1846 - 1848
Rev. James Anderton ....1848 - 1849
Rev. Daniel Herne...................................1849 - 1851
Rev. Thomas Spencer ....1851 - 1862
Very Rev. Dean Thomas Kelly ....1862 - 1887
Rt. Rev. Canon Patrick Louis Kelly ....1887 - 1922
Monsignor John O'Brien ....1922 - 1948
Rev. Patrick L. Kennedy ....1948 - 1965
Very Rev. Dean Thomas Winder ....1965 - 1975
Canon Michael Casey ....1975 - 1988
Rev. J. J. Kavanagh.................................1988 - 1993
Rev. Patrick McCambridge........................1993 - 2000
Rev. James Gallagher...............................2003 -

ST. JOAN OF ARC (founded 1926 as Chapel of Ease to St. James)
Rev. Herbert Vincent O'Neill ....1925 - 1958
Rev. Francis Patrick Duffy ....1958 - 1968
Rev William H. Doyle ....1968 - 1976
Rev. Patrick W. Murphy ....1976 - 1979
Rev. Brendan Flynn ....1979 - 1984
Rev. Colm Grogan ....1984 - 1987
Rev. Michael de Felice ....1987 -

ST. MONICA'S (founded 1923)
Rev. Benedict Cain ....1923 - 1929
Rev. Dr. John Foley ....1929 - 1948
Rev. Monsignor H. Fitzpatrick ....1948 - 1960
Rev. Hugh O'Donoghue ....1960 - 1985
Rev. Michael O'Connor............................1985 - 2001
Rev Pat Sexton.......................................2001 -

ST. ROBERT BELLARMINE'S (founded 1932)
Rev. Robert Coupe ....1932 - 1947
Rev. William Byrne ....1947 - 1954

Rev. James W. Byrne ....1954 - 1980
Rev. Noel O'Connell ....1980 - 1985
Rev. John O'Hara ....1985 - 1990
Rev. Edward Cain ....1990 - 2000
Rev. Patrick Harnett............................2000 -

ST. WINEFRIDE'S (founded 1895)
Rev. Henry Blanchard.........................1895 - 1946
Rev. Joseph McDowell ....1946 - 1965
Rev. P. Murphy ....1965 - 1971
Rev. Richard Firth...............................1971 - 1974
Rev. Bernard Wyche ....1974 - 1978
Rev. Philip Barnett..............................1978 - 1982
Rev. Patrick Ryan................................1982 - 1986
Rev. James Clarkson ....1986 - 2003
St. Winefride's and St. James' parishes amalgamate

■ NON-CONFORMIST CHURCHES AND CHAPELS IN BOOTLE, AND MINISTERS WHEN KNOWN

● METHODIST CHURCHES AND CHAPELS

PRIMITIVE METHODIST CHAPEL, QUEENS ROAD SHERIDAN PLACE (1883-1956)
Rev. T. Savage....................................1883 - 1885
Rev. R. Carr ....1885 - 1890
Rev J. D. Jackson................................1890 - 1901
Rev Thomas H. Hunt ....1901 - 1905
Rev. Richard W. Burnett......................1905 - 1915
Rev. Phillip J. Fisher...........................1915 - 1925

WESLEYAN METHODIST CHAPEL, SHERIDAN STREET (1848-1942)

WESLEYAN METHODIST READING ROOM, ANGLESEY STREET (1909-)

WESLEYAN METHODIST, BALLIOL ROAD (1865-1971)
Rev. Owen Jones.................................1870 - 1883
Rev G. Fowler.....................................1883 - 1888
Rev. Thomas Rogers ....1888 - 1893
Rev. W. Burchell ....1893 - 1895
Rev. Henry Bone ....1895 - 1901
Rev. Thomas J. Choate ....1901 - 1905
Rev. George Smith ....1905 - 1910
Rev. J. H. Carson ....1910 - 1914
Rev. E. Brentall ....1914 - 1915
Rev. John E. Mattinson ....1915 - 1920
Rev. Joseph K. Whitehead ....1920 - 1925
Rev Wilfred Hackett ....1925 - 1930
Rev. Owen Jones ....1930 - 1931
Rev. R. Peacock ....1931 - 1935
Rev. Philip Thompson ....1935 - 1952
Rev. E. Ralph Bates ....1952 - 1958
Rev. Edwin P. Sheppard.......................1958 - 1960
Rev. R.E. Cubbon ....1960 - 1965
Rev. J. A. Wilson ....1965 -

WELSH CALVINISTIC METHODIST CHURCH, BRASENOSE ROAD: STANLEY ROAD (1862-
Rev. Griffith Ellis...............................1875 - 1881
Rev John Clegg...................................1881 - 1915
Rev. Owen Lloyd Jones ....1915 - 1919
Rev. William Davies ....1920 - 1936
Rev. J. Wesley Felix ....1944 - 1951
Rev. R. Gele Williams (died 1959)...........1951 - 1957
Rev. T. Lawson ....1957 -

WELSH METHODIST CHURCH, TRINITY ROAD
John Robert Ellis................................1896 -
Rev. W. H. Hughes..............................1935 -

WELSH METHODIST CHURCH, CYPRUS ROAD
Rev. Thomas Kirkup ....1901 - 1910
Rev. J. C. Jowett ....1910 - 1913
Rev. J.E. Mattison..............................1913 - 1915
Rev. Thomas Penbale..........................1915 - 1920
Rev. Norman D. Thop ....1920 - 1925
Rev. Henry C. Veale............................1925 -

● PRESBYTERIAN CHURCHES AND CHAPELS

PRESBYTERIAN CHURCH OF WALES, STANLEY RD
Rev. Griffiths Ellis ....1873 - 1911
Rev. O. Lloyd Jones ....1911 - 1917
Rev. William Davies ....1917 - 1938
Rev. T. Tudor Jones............................1940 - 1942
Rev. Gele Williams ....1944 - 1954
Rev. W. Gray Edwards........................1957 - 1960
Mr. W.G. Hughes Edwards ....1960 - 1970
Rev. William Jones ....1970 -

WELSH PRESBYTERIAN CHURCH, PEEL ROAD
Rev. C. Currie Hughes ....1925 - 1031
Rev. Rowland Lloyd ....1931 - 1935

PRESBYTERIAN CHURCH (SCOTTISH), DERBY RD

DERBY ROAD PRESBYTETRIAN CHURCH(1850-1885)
Rev. W. M. Taylor...............................1855 - 1972
Rev Robert French ....1872 - 1872
Rev. A. Scott Matheson ....1873 - 1877
Rev. James Bodel.................................1877 - 1885
Church moves to Trinity Road.

TRINITY PRESBYTERIAN CHURCH (1885-1941)
Rev. James Bodel.................................1885 - 1916
Rev. George D. Walker ....1916 - 1919

Rev. William McIntosh Traill ....1920 - 1929
Rev. William George Humphrey ....1930 - 1933
Rev. Hugh Ridehalgh Jones............................1934 - 1939
Mr. T. Roberts Preacher in charge ....1940 - 1941
Rev. Emmanuel Mann ....1941 - 1943

ST. PAUL'S PRESBYT. CHURCH, PEEL ROAD (1884-1941)

Rev. James Hunter Collie ....1884 - 1906
Rev. Edward Augustus Elliott Burrows.............1907 - 1914
Rev. Edward Walter Toms ....1914 - 1920
Rev. John Gibson ....1920 - 1928
Rev. Cedric Charles Edward Mercer ....1929 - 1931
Rev. Nicol Grieve ....1931 - 1934
Lay Assistant V. J. Abernethy ....1934 - 1936
Lay Assistant Harry Buchanan Barrow ....1936 - 1938
Lay Assistant L. S. Leslie ....1938 - 1941
Church destroyed by bombing

ST. PAUL & TRINITY PRESBYT. CHURCH (1941-1980)

Rev. J. A. Whitcombe ....1941 - 1961
Rev. David J. Martin......................................1963 - 1976
The church demolished.

ENGLISH PRESBYTERIAN CHURCH SPRINGWELL ROAD

Between 1900-02 church at 5 Monfa Road.
Rev. Sidney B. Evans ....1902 - 1911
Rev. J. Howell Evans ....1911 - 1914
Pastor J. W. Jones ....1916 - 1918
Rev. J. C. Rowland ....1918 - 1924
Rev. D.V. Bundred ....1928 - 1933
Pastor Lawson...1934 - 1937
Rev. Joshua Davies (With Spellow Lane Church)...1938 - 1943
Rev Ewart Jenkins ....1945 - 1947
Rev. Rev. Archibald Brown ....1950 - 1957
Rev. J. J. Mathews ....1959 - 1974

Rev. Elwyn Jones...1974 - 1975
Church is linked with Clubmoor Church from 1978
Rev David Broster ....1978 - 1983
Rev Jonathan Sleigh ....1984 - 1986
Rev. Adrian Pratt..1987 - 1989
Rev. David Evans..1991 -

BOOTLE & LINACRE PRESBYTERIAN MISSION, LABURNUM PLACE (1858-1862)

THE PRESBYTERIAN INSTITUTE / LINACRE PARK PRESBYTERIAN CHURCH (1928-1972)

Pastor C.A. Cooke ....1928 - 1937
Pastor George W. Fauset.................................1937 - 1948
Pastor A. Franklin ....1949 - 1953
Pastor D.G.K. Johnston ....1954 - 1962
Pastor Vincent Fry ....1962 - 1964
Pastor Frank Askew ....1964 - 1967
Pastor Kenneth Jordan ....1968 - 1969
Pastor Michael Marshall ....1970 - 1972
In 1972 joined United Reformed Church to become

ST STEPHEN'S UNITED REFORMED CHURCH

Pastor Michael Marshall ....1972 - 1979
Rev. Mary Elizabeth Williamson Carrol.............1982 - 1993
Rev. Michael Marshall ....1993 -

● CONGREGATIONAL CHURCHES AND CHAPELS

EMMANUEL CONGREGATIONAL CHURCH, STANLEY RD.

Rev George P. Jarvis ....1876 - 1880
Rev. Thomas Dunlop ....1880 - 1915
Rev. John W. G. Ward.....................................1915 - 1920
Rev. Alfred William Anderson..........................1920 - 1925
Rev. Henry Francis Croft ....1925 - 1935
Rev. Stanley F. Sullivan ....1935 - 1960

Rev. Elfred J. Edwards ....1960 - 1965

MARSH STREET MISSION (1896)

CONGREGATIONAL CHURCH, MARSH LANE (1897)

● WELSH CONGREGATIONAL CHURCHES

WELSH CONGREGATIONAL CHURCH MERTON ROAD (1903-19)   BREEZE HILL (1969-1993)

Rev. W. D. Jones (former Free Church of the Welsh) 1923

WELSH CONGREGATIONAL CHURCH, BRASENOSE RD.

WELSH CONGREGATIONAL CHURCH, KNOWSLEY ROAD

WELSH CONGREGATIONAL CHURCH, MARSH LANE

Rev. John Hawan Rees ....1901 - 1905
John W. Griffiths (secretary).............................1910 - 1915
Rev. Albert Jones ....1915 - 1925
Rev. J. D. Evans..1925 - 1935
Rev. Brynmor Evans ....1935 - 1940

WELSH CONGREGATIONAL CHURCH, UNIVERSITY/TRINITY ROAD

Rev. W. Thomas ....1885 - 1905
Rev. Tudwell Williams......................................1905 - 1910
John Jones Secretary.......................................1910 - 1915
Rev. William Roberts.......................................1915 - 1925

WELSH CONGREGATIONAL CHURCH, RHYL STREET

● BAPTIST CHURCHES AND CHAPELS

**BOOTLE cum LINACRE MISSION (1862-1886)
WATERWORKS STREET moved to ASH STREET 1886
ASH STREET BAPTIST CHURCH 1886**

Lay Ministers J. W. Scholefield and R. J. Glasgow .1886 - 1914
Rev. A. T. Roberts ....1914 - 1918
Rev. H. J. Powell ....1919 - 1925
Rev. L. P. Cook ....1926 - 1934
Rev. Kenneth Hinchcliffe ....1934 - 1960
Rev. Percy Pople ....1960 - 1968
Rev. Dayson Burley ....1968 - 1975
Rev. David White..1975 - 1981
Rev. Brian Astill...1981 -

BAPTIST MISSION CHURCH, SUSSEX ST. (1887-1921)

BAPTIST CHURCH, DERBY ROAD (Chapel St. 1844-96)

Rev. R. H. Roberts ....1870 - 1875
Rev. W. H. Perkins...1875 - 1880
Rev Z. T. Dowen...1880 - 1885
Rev. W. C. Davies ....1885 - 1890
Rev. A. H. Smith ....1890 - 1896
Congregation move to new church in Stanley Road 1896
Rev. A. H. Smith ....1896 - 1905
Rev Rowland D. Lloyd ....1905 - 1918
Rev. Arthur John Kellam ....1918 - 1944
Pastor Harry Hughes...1944 - 1958
Deaconess Elva Weir Hulme ....1958 - 1968
*Church closes in 1968; congregation move to new church
in Fleetwoods Lane Netherton, which opened in 1969*
Deaconess Elva Weir Hulme ....1969 - 1970
Rev Roy Cave ....1970 - 1974
Rev. Douglas Burley ....1974 - 1978
Rev. Donald Samuel Page ....1978 - 1986
Pastor David Lathom ....1986 - 1996
Interregnum ....1996 - 2005
Rev. Allan I. Finnegan..2005

BETHAL BAPTIST CHURCH, SOUTHPORT ROAD (1934

Pastor Edward Jeffries ....1934 - 1935
Rev. Anderson Brown...1935 - 1949
Rev. James Mair...1950 - 1960
Pastor Ernest Frier ....1960 - 1968
Rev. Keith Barker ....1968 - 1980
Rev. Ian Paterson ....1985 -

● **WELSH BAPTIST CHURCHES AND CHAPELS**

WELSH BAPTIST CHURCH, BRASENOSE ROAD 1871

Pastor John Davies...1880 - 1885
Pastor John Henry Hughes ....1890 - 1898
Church moves to new building in Balliol Road in 1898
Rev. Peter Williams ....1898 - 1925
Rev. Peter Jones ....1925 - 1935
Rev. William R. Jones ....1935 - 1944

**WELSH BAPTIST CHAPEL, KNOWSLEY ROAD
(1882-1898)**

Pastor L. W. Lewis...1890 - 1910

**WELSH MISSION HAWTHORNE ROAD 1916-1960
closed and becomes part of PEEL ROAD WELSH
CHURCH**

**WELSH BAPTIST CHAPEL, RHYL STREET (1887-
1898)**

● **UNITARIAN CHUCHES AND CHAPELS**

UNITARIAN FREE CHURCH, STANLEY ROAD (1894-

Rev. Walter Short ....1913 - 1925
Rev. H. Fisher Short ....1925 - 1940

**UNITARIAN MISSION HALL WATERWORKS
STREET (1909)**

■ **UNDENOMINATIONAL HALLS AND CHAPELS**

OLIVET MISSION HALL, MARSH LANE (1909)

**BOOTLE & LINACRE UNDENOMINATIONAL
MISSION, LINACRE LANE 1862, NEW STREET
1870, WATERWORKS STREET 1871-1882**

**EBENEZER MISSION HALL FOR CARTERS,
BRASENOSE ROAD (1877)**

NORTHFIELD GOSPEL HALL (1938

PROTESTANT FREE CHURCH, TRINITY ROAD

Rev. H. Fisher Short 1927
Rev. John Franklin .... - 1970
Rev. Brian Astill..1971 - 1975
Pastor Ernest Frier ....1975 -

**BANK HALL MISSION STANLEY ROAD
LIVERPOOL (1905)**

No Pastor until 1937. (Interregnums 39-46; 75-79; 85-88)
Rev. L. H. Nuttall...1937 - 1939
Rev Thomas Lawson ....1946 - 1971
Rev. R. T. Gray ....1971 - 1975
Church relocates to Knowsley Road in 1976.
Rev. R. T. Gray ....1976 - 1979
Rev. Robert Watson ....1979 - 1985
Rev. Derek Drapper ....1988 - 1995
Rev. Paul Kinnard..2005 -

SALVATION ARMY CITADEL, STANLEY ROAD (1954)

■ **JEHOVAH'S WITNESSES KINGDOM HALL, PARK
STREET (1954)**

Bibliography

MAIN SOURCES

Bootle School Board Minutes 1870-1903

Bootle Education Committee Minutes 1903-1974

Kelly's Directory of Liverpool and District 1850-1970

Liverpool Red Book 1900-1970

Liverpool Diocesan Directory 1900-1970

Crockford's Clerical Directory: various dates 1935-2005

Archdiocese of Liverpool Directory: various dates 1900-2002

Bootle Times newspaper 1870-1974

Borough of Bootle Mayors' Scrapbooks 1895-1915

Bootle County Borough Handbooks/Guides 1940s-1970s

Bootle Municipal Government Centenary Celebrations Handbook 1935

Bootle County Borough Education Committee: booklets to mark the opening of schools and other educational establishments.

Maps of Bootle covering the period 1763 to 1998

Municipal Year Book and Diary: various dates 1900-1948

OTHER WORKS

Brookes R. Never a Dull Moment: the Bootle Story [1968]

Flynn W. St James Church Centenary 1886-1986 [1986]

Herington P. Bootle in Times Past [1970]

Jones J. The Welsh Builders on Merseyside [1946]

Lacy F. Strange Story of the Bootle Corporation Fraudulent Bonds [1994]

Lamb C. Story of Bootle to circa 1850 [undated]

Latham E. History and Bootle [1999]

McDermott L. Orrell, Doorway to the Past [1989]

Marsh B & Almond S. Home Port: Bootle, the Blitz and the Battle of the Atlantic [1993]

Redman R. & Sands C. History of Christ Church Bootle [1980]

Redman R. & Sands C. Bootle Signposts: history and directory of Bootle streets [2003]

Regan M. Children of Bootle (a socio-medical history) [1968]

Richards C. St Mary's C of E School 1835-1985 [1985]

Woolley P. Bootle: a portrait in old picture postcards [1987]

Woolley P. Bootle: archive photographs [1996]

Woolley P. Bootle: a second portrait in old picture postcards [1988]

Woolley P. Bootle: the second selection [2001]

Woolley P. Bootle and Orrell [2001]

Acknowledgements

We would like to put on record our appreciation for the help given to us during our research by Mark Sargant, Senior Development Manager (Local History) and his staff based at Crosby Library; Keith Cawdron of Church House, for assistance with details of Anglican clergy; and Dr Meg Whittle, Archdiocesan Archivist, for assistance with Roman Catholic clergy. Thanks are also due to the many headteachers and officers of Sefton's Education Department who have generously spared time to help us fill in the missing pieces of the complicated jigsaw of school development and staff changes. Finally a thank you to our wives, Valerie and Barbara, without whose support and encouragement this project would never have reached fruition.